THE ATLANTIC CRITICAL REVIEW

QUARTERLY

A Peer Reviewed Journal Indexed in
MLA Directory of Periodicals

JULY – SEPTEMBER 2015

VOLUME 14 NUMBER 3

ATLANTIC

PUBLISHERS & DISTRIBUTORS (P) LTD

CONTRIBUTORS

Amar Nath Prasad, Associate Professor & Head, Department of English, Jagdam College, J.P. University, Chhapra, Bihar.

Anita Myles, Professor of English, DDU Gorakhpur University, Gorakhpur, Uttar Pradesh.

Arindam Das, Assistant Professor (Dept. of Humanities), Heritage Institute of Technology, Kolkata, West Bengal.

Basavaraj Naikar, Professor & Chairman, Department of English, Karnatak University, Dharwad, Karnataka.

Billy Bin Feng Huang. Ph.D. Candidate, National Jengji University, Taipei, Taiwan (R.O.C.).

Gauri Shankar Jha, Head, Department of English, Indira Gandhi Govt. College, TEZU, Arunachal Pradesh.

Goutam Ghosal, Professor of English, Visva-Bharati, Santiniketan, West Bengal.

Indrajeet Mishra, Assistant Professor, Department of English DAV PG College, Varanasi, Uttar Pradesh.

Mahima Singh, Guest Lecturer, DAV PG College, Varanasi, Uttar Pradesh.

N. Sharada Iyer, Head, Department of English, Vasanta College for Women, Rajghat, Varanasi, Uttar Pradesh.

Norah Nivedita Shaw, Associate Professor, Department of English, Sri Arvind Mahila College, Patna, Bihar.

Pallavi Singh, Research Scholar, Ranchi University, Ranchi, Jharkhand.

Samira Sinha, Assistant Professor, Department of English, J.N. College, Ranchi University, Ranchi, Jharkhand.

Sumathi Shivakumar, Assistant Professor of English, A.M. Jain College, Chennai.

THE ATLANTIC CRITICAL REVIEW
VOLUME 14 NUMBER 3 (JULY-SEPTEMBER 2015)

CONTENTS

If Only He Were A Flâneur—On How Art and Commodity Bewitch Paul and His Experiences with the Crowd in Willa Cather's "Paul's Case"

BILLY BIN FENG HUANG

> The viewpoint of the detective is, like that of the flâneur, panoramic.... Like the flâneur, he removes and distances himself from what he observes in order to achieve his panoramic perspective....
>
> Dana Brand, "From the Flâneur to the Detective: Interpreting the City of Poe", 237.

"PAUL'S Case" is one of Willa Cather's best known, or perhaps the most frequently anthologized stories. It first appeared in her collection of stories called *The Troll Garden* in 1905. Unlike most of Cather's stories, the settings of the story are two modern cities, Pittsburg and New York. Based on an actual suicide of a high school student in the Pittsburgh area where Cather used to live, "Paul's Case" describes how Paul, a high school student with a sensitive temperament, eventually loses himself and commits suicide. As far as Paul is concerned, "anything associated with the world of art is beautiful and inspiring" (Arnold, *Critical Survey*, 452). In this story, what is associated with the world of art is not only art works but also glittering, high-class commodity. And it is precisely Paul's inclination to get obsessed with them that is responsible for his death. On the other hand, the flâneur[1] is one of the key figures in Walter Benjamin's *The Arcades Project*. Dana Brand describes the flâneur as a sharp observer of the urban. Lutz Koepnick further states, "The flâneur Baudelaire understands how to parry the multiplicity of stimuli in urban life. He also knows how to use the transformation of the cortex as a source of aesthetic pleasure and artistic productivity" (*Walter Benjamin,* 148). Evidently, a flâneur is supposed to resist the superficial beauty of the urban life, from the course of which he may even derive tremendous pleasure. In this paper, I intend to do a contrastive analysis of Paul and a flâneur. To be more specific, unlike most research papers where similarities are examined, my paper aims to differentiate Paul from a flâneur, even though there may be some verisimilitude between them every now and then. By investigating the discrepancies between them, I attempt to account for how art and commodity bewitch Paul as well as his experiences with the crowd in New York. Ultimately, I hope to decipher Paul's tragic suicide.

In "Paul's Case," Paul apparently does everything he can to emulate a dandy. For instance, in the beginning of the story, when Paul's father "confessed his perplexity about his son" at the principal's office, "Paul entered the faculty room suave and smiling…but for all that, there was something of the dandy about him, and he wore an opal pin in his neatly knotted black four-in-hand, and a red carnation in his button hole" (*Willa Cather,* 468). John H. Randall thinks of it as a symbol of Paul's alienation from the world (*The Landscape,* 275). In her "Is Cather's Paul a Case," Loretta Wasserman views this red carnation as "the badge of Paul's fidelity to his dream". She points out that it is symbolic of "the inarticulate boy's dim sense of a beauty connected to substance and reality but not available to him" (206). That is, only by wearing this red carnation can give Paul an illusory identity as a dandy. Or we can say that as far as Paul is concerned, it is a weak embodiment of an ideal, dandy-like life that seems unattainable in reality. Pretending to be a dandy, Paul has taken a great interest in art. For example, one night Paul is on duty as an usher at Carnegie Hall.

> When he reached the concert hall the doors were not yet open. It was chilly outside, and he decided to go up into the picture gallery—always deserted at this hour—where there were some of Raffelli's gay studies of Paris streets and an airy blue Venetian scene or two that always exhilarated him…Paul possessed himself of the place and walked confidently up and down, whistling under his breath. After a while he sat down before a blue Rico and lost himself. (470)

And during the concert, Paul "lost himself as he had done before the Rico". And "the first sigh of the instruments seemed to free some hilarious spirit within him" (471). Sharon O'Brien notes that Paul's love for music and theater brings about his distaste for the mundane and the conventional (*Willa Cather*, 283). That is, art and music have bewitched Paul so much that Paul is almost completely cut off from the outer world. With such a bewitchment of art and music, Paul has driven himself into a fantastic world of his own creation, refusing to step out.

As I've mentioned previously, the reason why Paul is fascinated with the glittering world of art and music is that he likes to fantasize about being a dandy. In *Walter Benjamin: Critical Constellations*, Graeme Gilloch uses the term "flâneur-as-dandy" in describing the flâneur's pursuit of urban fashions (132)[2]. However, even though a flâneur may seem to be a dandy like Paul, he views art from a unique perspective:

> Trace and aura. The trace is appearance of a nearness, however far removed the thing that left it behind may be. The aura is appearance of a distance, however close the thing that calls it forth. In the trace, we gain possession of the thing: in the aura, it takes possession of us. (*Arcades Project,* M16a.4)

In Convolute M of *The Arcades Project,* Benjamin draws this distinction between trace and aura. He asserts that a true flâneur will capture art works' trace rather than their aura. First, Benjamin has attempted to define aura a number of times. In "The Work of Art," Benjamin has given it such a definition, "What is aura actually? A strange weave of time: the unique appearance or semblance of distance, no matter how close the object may be" (*Selected Writings,* 518). On the other hand, Benjamin has also stated that aura is a particular power an image or object possesses by virtue of its singularity, authenticity. And it is "the unique phenomenon of distance however close it may be" (*Illuminations,* 224-25). There is one thing about aura we can be certain of: aura is meant to maintain the distance between art works and spectators. S. Brent Plate, in his *Walter Benjamin, Religion, and Aesthetics,* elaborates on Benjamin's conception of aura:

> Aura depends on a metaphysical distance from an object even though it may be physically close. Critically, the aura is not inherent in the object itself but is built up around the object through history and through social conditions…the object is made to seem untouchable. (88)

Plate clarifies that aura is a metaphysical distance that makes an object unapproachable. Unlike physical distance, such a metaphysical distance won't go away in spite of one's nearness to the object. In other words, it is the authority of an art work. "Even if the art work were only inches from the viewer's eyes, there would still be the feeling of a gulf separating viewer from object" (Nichols, "The End of Aura?," 256). Gilloch further points out that the authority aura endows with art works can actually be traced back to their 'cult value,' "The aura possessed by the work of art today is the last vestige of this original cult value" (184). Gilloch's observation explains why Benjamin says that aura "takes possession of us." Aura puts a metaphysical distance between an art work and its viewers so that the former can be worshipped by the latter. Only in this way can the art work serve its ritualistic purposes, and above all, enchant its viewers. On the other hand, it's fair to say that the workings of trace seem quite the opposite to those of aura. According to Benjamin, it is a nearness in spite of the physical distance between the object and the viewer. Gilloch articulates for the "proximity, tactility and decipherment" of trace, thinking that it "bears witness to the dissolution of the object" and "is intimately connected to the transient, ruinous realm of allegorical expression" (183). That is to say, trace offers one, an opportunity to get intimately connected with the object until it gets deciphered allegorically. Therefore, if one captures the trace of an object, (s)he can "gain possession of" it, as Benjamin has put it.

For some critics, the distinction between aura and trace may be blurred from time to time. For instance, Gilloch does propose to view "aura as trace" or "the trace as aura" (183). In discussing, or perhaps problematizing the Benjaminian notion of aura, Siegfried J. Schimdt states, "Sacred objects are not only objects at a distance from our everyday lives; by establishing that distance they also attract and intensify a desire to touch" ("From Aura-Loss to Cyberspace," 85). In other words, Schimdt doesn't think aura is synonymous with distance. Instead, he believes that aura, like trace, can be correlated with tactility as well. However, in the case of Paul, the distinction between aura and trace remains hard and fast. Clearly, as Paul gets exhilarated by Raffelli's studies of Paris and Venice, or loses himself before the blue Rico, he is utterly bedazzled by the aura of the art works no matter how close he attempts to get to them. Unable to capture their trace, Paul has never possessed them because he is so distanced by their aura.[3]

So far I have pinpointed the first major difference between the flâneur and Paul: the former captures the trace while the latter gets captivated by the aura. However, my emphasis here is more than that. First of all, I would like to delve into the root cause of this bewitchment. Apparently, Paul is attracted to the glamorous world of music, the theater, and art because he desires the beautiful things money can buy (*Short Stories for Students,* 195). Besides, in "Paul's Case," Paul's upstairs room has "horrible yellow wallpaper, the creaking bureau with the greasy plush collar-box, and over his painted wooden bed the pictures of George Washington and John Calvin" (473). Marilyn Arnold believes that Paul wants to make his way into "the world of wealth and glamour;" therefore, George Washington and John Calvin stand for the spirits of the American dream shared by the "various chiefs and overlords whom Paul would like to emulate" (*Willa Cather's Short Fiction,* 62-63). In other words, as Paul wears the red carnation to assume an imaginary identity as a dandy, he is drawn to art and music, or perhaps put under the spell of their aura, simply because it is the only way he can identify with the capitalists or business tycoons he has looked up to. In commenting on the creation of aura, Plate highlights its origin:

> In this play of proximity and distance at the heart of the aura is the issue of *who* is in control of the relation. Quite simply, the class for which art is created supplies the traditional values of art and aesthetics, which up until the twentieth century was strictly the governing class.... The authority eventually shifted away from the church to the bourgeoisie.... This class of people created its own legitimating cultural authority, utilizing aura as a tool of legitimation.... (91-92)

Plate points out that the crux of the issue of aura is actually the power structure. That is, as art is created solely for the governing class, it stands to reason that the governing class is responsible for the creation of its aura. Under such circumstances, the governing class can even manipulate aura to its own end. In the twentieth century, the bourgeoisie has taken the position of the governing class, or the controller of aura. Plate's viewpoint does help us to account for why Paul gets bewitched by art and music. Idolizing the celebrities of the bourgeoisie class, Paul is deeply immersed in the bourgeoisie ideology. That's why he has fallen for the bourgeoisie-based aura of art and music so easily.

Later in "Paul's Case," Paul embezzles 1000$ from Denny & Carson and absconds to New York, where he checks into the Waldorf hotel. With the 1000$, Paul is eventually able to live a life he's been dreaming about. The minute he gets to New York, he begins shopping for all the accessories a dandy requires until "he was exactly the kind of boy he had always wanted to be" (482). His appearance may resemble a dandy's or a flâneur's a lot more in New York; however, he doesn't share the same urban experiences as a flâneur does. In New York, while Paul is strolling on the street, he attempts to blend in with the crowd:

> Above, about, within it all, was the rumble and roar, the hurry and the toss of thousands of human beings as hot for pleasure as himself, and on every side of him towered the glaring affirmation of the omnipotence of wealth.... He had no special desire to meet or to know any of these people; all he demanded was the right to look on and conjecture, to watch the pageant. (483-44)

It will appear as if Paul has successfully integrated himself into the crowd because "these were his own people" (483). Philip Page thinks that "Paul has created a fictional vision of New York that fits well enough with external reality so that he can live out his dream." Above all, his self-image is congruent with this external reality; in New York, "Paul has only one role to play...and...the disjointed fragments of his life have been temporarily welded together" ("The Theatricality," 555). In other words, Paul chooses to see what he wants to see in New York, and it's the same case scenario when Paul is in the crowd. In the crowd, Paul only sees these people's hunger for corporeal pleasures as well as their dazzling wealth; for Paul, the crowd in New York constitutes a pageant that "was a wonderful stage winter-piece" and "blossomed thus unnaturally in the snow" (482). Paul has envisioned a dream world in the crowd; he sees the crowd as a sparkling emblem of wealth because it is how he pictures New York in his dream. This is also why Paul fits in with the crowd because it makes him feel that his dream is materializing. As far as Paul is concerned, it is simply the only part he feels obligated to play in the crowd.

However, when the flâneur is walking among the crowd, he has completely different experiences than Paul. First, Baudelaire thinks that for the flâneur, "the crowd is his element, as the air is that of birds and water of fishes. His passion and profession are to become one flesh with the crowd" (*The Painter of Modern Life,* 9). Edmund White, citing Baudelaire, concludes that the flâneur should be compared to a mirror "as huge as the crowd—or to a kaleidoscope...that at every shake of the tube copies the configuration of multifarious life and the graceful movement of all its elements" (*The Flâneur*, 37). On the other hand, when it comes to walking in the crowd, Benjamin distinguishes a flâneur from a *badaub* or a rubberneck, "The average flâneur...is always in full possession of his individuality, while that of the rubberneck disappears, absorbed by the external world...which moves him to the point of intoxication and ecstasy" (*Arcades Project,* M6.5). That is, it is true that a flâneur is mingling with the crowd; paradoxically, he is also putting some distance between himself and the crowd at the same time to make sure that his individuality won't be compromised, just as Benjamin states, "And however much one may be aware that this isolation of the individual…is the fundamental principle of our society everywhere" (*Arcades Project,* M5a.1). Basically, it is the know-how of a flâneur when he is in a crowd, and it is also how he stays in possession of his individuality. Gilloch points out, "The flâneur is in the crowd but not of it…the flâneur is precisely the aloof individual who regards the crowd with aristocratic contempt…" (214). It is another major difference between Paul and a flâneur: Paul seems to truly become a part of the crowd because he "had no special desire to meet or to know any of these people". However, Paul never possesses any individuality in the crowd, nor does he know-how to distance himself from the crowd. Feasting his eyes on every possible sign of the omnipotent wealth, he is utterly intoxicated in the crowd. In this respect, Paul seems closer to the rubberneck than to the flâneur. (However, on second thought, we can easily see the difference between Paul and the *badaub*. For Benjamin, "the true rubberneck deserves the admiration of all upright and sincere hearts" because "his naïve soul aglow, ever inclined to reverie" (*Arcades Project*, M6.5). If Paul had a naïve soul or deserved any admiration, he wouldn't steal the 1000$ from Denny & Carson!

In addition, Paul's look in the crowd is another major problematic. In the crowd, Paul "had no special desire to meet or to know any of these people; all he demanded was the right to look on and conjecture, to watch the pageant." Sherry Crabtree notes that Paul "remains merely a spectator in this fairy tale land, even as he roams the street…" ("Cather's PAUL'S CASE," 207). That is, Paul only wishes to look because for him either New York or the crowd is a spectacle magnificent enough satiate his hunger to gaze. However, Benjamin has a much more sophisticated theorization about a flâneur's look and looked-at-ness.

> The city is the realization of that ancient dream of humanity, the labyrinth. It is this reality to which the flâneur, without knowing it, devotes himself…the flâneur has made a study of the physiognomic appearance of people in order to discover their nationality and social station, character and destiny, from a perusal of their gait, build, and play of features. (*Arcades Project,* M6a.4)

In short, the flâneur has a physiognomic look. For Benjamin, the flâneur's look can be so sharp that he is like a detective, "Preformed in the figure of the flâneur is that of the detective…an observer who will not let the unsuspecting malefactor out of his sight" (*Arcades Project,* M13a.2). David Frisby points out that a flâneur conducts his investigation by observing and reading the metropolis ("The Flâneur in Social Theory," 82). Rob Shields also adds a footnote to how a flâneur resembles a detective, "The flâneur is like a detective seeking clues who reads people's characters not only from the physiognomy of their faces but via a social physiognomy of the streets" ("Fancy footwork: Walter Benjamin's notes on flâneurie," 63). For Shields, a true flâneur is looking physiognomically at both people's faces and streets all the time. On the other hand, Benjamin has contrived the "dialectic of the flâneurie": "on one side, the man who feels himself viewed by all and sundry as a true suspect and, on the other hand, the man who is utterly undiscoverable, the hidden man. Presumably, it is this dialectic that is developed in "The Man of the Crowd"" (*Arcades Project,* M2.8). Benjamin's so-called "dialectic of the flâneurie" is how the flâneur remains unseen when being looked at. Summing up a flâneur's look and looked-at-ness, Gilloch states that a flâneur is to see and to be seen while he is ambling and observing (214). Such an analysis helps to discriminate Paul from a true flâneur. As Crabtree suggests, when Paul is looking around in the crowd, he is merely a spectator of "the pageant" of New York city; namely, what he sees is "the rumble and roar, the hurry and the toss of thousands of human beings as hot for pleasure as himself." He is no detective at all, for he doesn't care to peruse these people's "gait, build, and play of features," let alone "discover their nationality and social station, character and destiny." Therefore, what he is looking at is a far cry from a physiognomic study. Besides, in the crowd, Paul "felt now that his surroundings explained him…he only had to glance down at his dress coat to reassure himself that here it would be impossible for anyone to humiliate him" (484). It would appear that Paul is moving undiscovered in the crowd. However, Paul's only concern is whether or not he's been dressed the way the crowd would consider appropriate. This is also the only reason for Paul's undiscoveredness: the crowd seems to have taken him in. Even so, it is still a blatant defiance of Benjamin's "dialectic of the flâneurie," for Paul is not "a suspect viewed by all and sundry," nor does he have any looked-at-ness.

In Benjamin's opinion, the crowd could also be a veil for the flâneur:

> The masses in Baudelaire. They stretch before the flâneur as a veil: they are the newest drug for the solitary.... Finally, within the labyrinth of the city, the masses are the newest and most inscrutable labyrinth. Through them, previously unknown chthonic traits are imprinted on the image of the city. (*Arcades Project,* M16.3)

In the quoted passage, Benjamin aims at how a flâneur deciphers the urban landscape while he is walking in the crowd. "The crowd is the veil through which the familiar city beckons to the flâneur as phantasmagoria—now a landscape, now a room," as Benjamin states in the Exposé (of 1935) of *The Arcades Project* (10). That is, for the flâneur, the masses or the crowd constitutes a labyrinth, in which he develops a phantasmagoric vision. With it, the flâneur can see the city as "the intoxicated interpenetration of street and residence" (*Arcades Project,* M3a.5). Or he can transform the city into "one great interior—a house whose rooms are the *quartiers*, no less clearly demarcated by thresholds than are real rooms" or "a landscape in the round" (*Arcades Project,* M3.2). Namely, with the crowd as the veil on a flâneur's face, the city seems like a demarcated room or an open space. Above all, such a phantasmagoric vision is supposed to help the flâneur to interpret the previously unknown dark traits of the city. For Benjamin, the flâneur is "a predatory, privileged reader of the metropolitan environment". For him, the city is a "semiological universe to be deciphered" (Gilloch, 219). Therefore, deciphering the urban landscape, the flâneur must catch sight of the previously unseen sides of the modern city.[4]

As I've mentioned previously, what he sees in the crowd is the omnipotence of wealth in New York:

> The snow was falling faster, lights streamed from the hotels that reared their many stories fearlessly up into the storm, defying the raging Atlantic winds. A long, black stream of carriages poured down the avenue, intersected here and there by other streams, tending horizontally. (482)

This is the urban landscape of New York for Paul, namely, an everlasting affluence that can stand any tough test. Jennifer Hicks points out, "Yet Paul is so entranced in his fairy world [*ie, New York*] that he believes it is where he has always been, and that is why he feels so at peace with himself..." ("Paul's Case," 203, *italics mine*). Paul chooses to see New York as a fairy land of wealth, so it conveniently becomes the focus of his vision in the crowd, which certainly differentiates Paul from a true flâneur. True as it may be, I intend to take my analysis to a higher level. Ursula Link-Heer quotes Benjamin's sentence, "The one seen or believing oneself to be seen gazes up," to elaborate on his complex ideas about "a resistance to this objectification of the apparatus [*ie, the camera*]" ("Aura Hysterica or the Lifted Gaze of the Object," 120, *italics mine*). Of course, it is definitely not the direction in which my analysis will go. Here, I would like to interpret this sentence rather literally, applying it to the case of Paul. As mentioned above, Paul believes himself to be seen in the crowd, so he gazes at the people around him, in the course of which he only cares about if his clothing is fit for New York, a fantastic, money-flooded land. We have to note that the basic logic behind Paul's gaze is his paranoiac belief in his dandy appearance, or if we want to put it more bluntly, his (stolen) wealth. As Edward W. Pitcher points out New York is a land of "Romance and Magic for Paul. In this world…magic is money and money is magic" ("Paul's Case," 548). Evidently, such a conviction is imposed on Paul by capitalist society, for "the American dream of wealth might have corrupted Paul, fostering in him a love of materialism which leads to his ruin" (*Short Stories for Students,* 196). Therefore, with such a false, given ideology, no wonder Paul's vision becomes so narrow in the crowd. Discussing a flâneur in the crowd, Gilloch asserts that as the flâneur watches the crowd and becomes a member of it, the "spectator and spectacle coincide". Above all, the vision of the flâneur provocatively prefigures that of the social theorist (244). Evidently, such a prefiguration is due to how the flâneur manages to see the whole social ambience. Paul, unlike the flâneur, has, or perhaps we should say, is given a limited vision. Hence, he fails to see in perspective either New York or its crowd. It is also at this point where he loses his individuality.

It is also worthwhile to investigate how commodity has bewitched Paul. As soon as Paul arrives at New York, he has a cabman drive him to a men's furnishing establishment. There, he spends two hours shopping.

> His new street suit he put on in the fitting-room; the frock coat and dress clothes he had bundled into the cab with his new shirts. Then he drove to a hatter's and a shoe house. His next errand was at Tiffany's, where he selected silver mounted brushes and a pin…. Lastly, he stopped at a trunk shop on Broadway, and had his purchases packed into various traveling bags. (480)

And in the fancy dining-room of the Waldorf hotel, Paul "sat down at a table near a window. The flowers, the white linen, the many-colored win glasses, the gay toilette of the women...all flooded Paul's dream with bewildering radiance" (483). It is plain to see that Paul is unable to resist the luxuries New York has to offer, for they are the only link between Paul and his fantasy, as Michael N. Salda points out, "He[*Paul*] finds himself delighting in each article of new clothing and basking in the luxury of a dream world..." ("What Really Happens in "Paul's Case,"" 117, *italics mine*). In some respect, Paul has even fetishized the commodity. The flâneur also goes in for, or has an inclination to fetishize fashionable commodity. Gilloch states that the arcade is "home to the fetishized commodity...[*and*] the whirl of fashion..." (133, *italics mine*). Margaret Cohen is more specific when arguing that Benjamin, following "the utopian socialist Fourier," believes that the arcade has "facilitated the blurring of boundaries between human and commodity, thereby producing the allure of the commodity fetishism" ("Benjamin's Phantasmagoria," 212). In addition, Gilloch regards the arcade as "a favorite haunt of the flâneur" (132), or "the theatricality of the dandified flâneur" (133). Seemly, it stands to reason to associate the flâneur with commodity fetishism. However, by no means can we say that it's something Paul and the flâneur have in common. Here, the key lies in clarifying how Benjamin correlates a flâneur to commodity:

> Empathy with the commodity is fundamentally empathy with exchange value. The flâneur is the virtuoso of this empathy. He takes the concept of market ability itself for a stroll. Just as his final ambit is the department store, his last incarnation is the sandwich-man. (*Arcades Project,* M17a.2)

In this passage, it is the sequentiality that we should focus on. When Benjamin says that a flâneur's "final ambit is the department store," and that "his last incarnation is the sandwich-man," he seems to imply that commodity fetishism will eventually triumph over the flâneur. That is, capitalism will at last impose its new order on the metropolis; it is at this point where flâneurie will become a desperate attempt to fill the emptiness of commodity even though it is actually a resignation to it (Tester, Introduction, *The Flâneur,* 13). However, it does not occur until the flâneur is fully acquainted with the exchange value of commodity or "takes the concept of market ability itself for a stroll". That is, a flâneur must know the ins and outs of commodity first.[5] This is why Benjamin also describes a flâneur as "the observer of the marketplace". "His knowledge is akin to the occult science of industrial fluctuations.

He is a spy for the capitalists, on assignment in the realm of consumers" (*Arcades Project,* M5,6). Gilloch thinks the flâneur is more of a blasé browser than a consumer (132) simply because a flâneur is equipped with a thorough understanding the commodity market.

Indeed, commodity fetishism has overwhelmed Paul. However, in contrast to a flâneur, Paul only has an immature understanding of commodity, and apparently, this half-baked understanding originates from his environment. Paul grows up on Cordelia Street, a place Paul thinks is full of "fagged looking business men," "sickening men, with combings of children's hair always hanging to their coats, and the smell of cooking in their clothes" (483). Yet there, "he rather liked to hear these legends of the iron kings, that were told and retold on Sundays and holidays…and he was interested in the triumphs of cash boys who had become famous, though he had no mind for the cash-boy stage" (476). "Paul despises the monotonous lives led by Cordelia Street residents, who believe that if they work hard, they too might lead such glamorous lives. But Paul shares their same desire: to become rich and lead a life without worry" (*Short Stories for Students,* 196). The residents of Cordelia Street have kept feeding Paul with these success stories until getting rich becomes Paul's only obsession. It is under such circumstances that Paul has developed his commodity fetishism. Paul's rudimentary knowledge of luxurious commodity is that it's the hallmark of the glamorous rich life he's been eager for, so just as he has been bewitched by art, Paul is enchanted by commodity as well. Therefore, a flâneur's understanding of commodity or capitalism is far beyond Paul's; Paul is a far cry from "the observer of the marketplace" or "a spy for the capitalists!"

Here, it's about time that I drew a sub-conclusion. As I've stated in the beginning of the paper, I aim to contrast Paul with a true flâneur. My point here is that the gap between Paul and a flâneur is precisely the abyss Paul tragically falls into: if only Paul were a flâneur, he could avoid the bourgeoisie-manipulated aura of art works; that is, he wouldn't associate them with a life of affluence. If only he were a flâneur, he could see the true nature of commodity; that is, he wouldn't take a fetishistic attitude towards the luxuries. If only he were a flâneur, he could peruse every inch of New York and its crowd; that is, New York shouldn't seem like a magical city of money. In brief, if only Paul were a flâneur, he might not have such a materialistic fantasy about his future. Their verisimilitudes and differences can be summarized in the diagram below:

The Verisimilitudes of Paul & a flâneur	
1. their dandified appearances and pursuit of urban fashions 2. their attraction to the crowd 3. commodity fetishism	
The differences between Paul & a flâneur	
Paul	A flâneur
1. the mere ability to capture art works' aura.	1. the ability to capture art works' trace.
2. the full integration of himself into the crowd; only cares whether his clothing is good enough for the crowd.	2. in full possession of his own individuality while blending in with the crowd; the crowd as a veil.
3. completely surrender to commodity fetishism; only has a rudimentary knowledge of capitalism.	3. must know the ins and outs of capitalism first.

Doubtless, this diagram aims to clarify the pivot of my paper: on the surface, Paul and a flâneur do bear certain resemblance; however, in actuality they are in stark contrast. Above all, it is their differences that lead straight to Paul's tragic suicide. (That's precisely why I've entitled my paper "If Only He Were A Flâneur" rather than "By no Means is Paul A Flâneur!")

At the end of "Paul's Case," Paul commits suicide by jumping in front of an approaching train. Before his suicide, "the carnations in his coat were drooping with the cold, he noticed; all their red glory over" (487). Then, "Paul took one of the blossoms carefully from his coat and scooped a little hole in the snow, where he covered it up" (488). Here, the cold, lifeless external world is contrasted with the ephemeral quality of his life or dream symbolized by his carnations. Ritually burying the blossom, he actually buries himself as well as his dream (Page, 556). With his fantasy shattered, Paul has to return to the colorless life on Cordelia Street, and death becomes his only permanent escape (Crabtree, 208). It is logical to say that Paul's materialistic fantasy is the root cause of his suicide. Above all, in examining Paul's 'un-flâneurie,' I have repeatedly argued that Paul's beliefs in materialism must come from his capitalistic surroundings. Hence, his suicide has to be brought about environmentally. Hermoine Lee suggests that Cather has seen the "horror of feckless, self-destructive Bohemianism". Then she composes this story so that readers can be absorbed into Paul's dream-world (*Willa Cather,* 77). Susan Rosowski suggests that the central theme of "Paul's Case" is the danger of Paul's imagination. And "without talent or ambition to perform, he is forever separated from the glittering world he seeks to enter, yet just as separated from the common world he seeks to leave" (*The Voyage Perilous,* 28). Both their analyses have failed to answer a focal question: where does Paul's dream-world or imagination come from? Hicks has cautioned us, "We need to remember, though, that Paul is an adolescent" (203). And an adolescent has to inherit his philosophy of life from the outer environment. Even Jane Nardin, arguing that Paul's homosexuality has resulted in his death, also has to admit that consumer-capitalism primarily accounts for Paul's actions ("Homosexual Identities," 42). Pitcher splendidly compares Paul to Faust, arguing that it is this Mephistophelean capitalist world that bargains with Paul for his soul, and finally wins it (547). In discussing Paul's death, either Nardin or Pitcher believes that capitalism is to blame. Concurring with them, I think Paul's 'un-flâneurie,' ascribable to capitalism, is responsible for Paul's suicide.

Exploring "Benjamin's actuality," Irving Wohlfarth states, "Actuality, thus conceived, is a matter of actualizing the specific potential of this particular now" ("The Measure of the Possible," 14). This is perhaps what Paul does in "Paul's Case". He "actualizes the potential" of the moment he sees the 1000$ because he wants to fulfill his dream, no matter how absurd it seems. On the other hand, the flâneur, "Benjamin's own self-ideal" (Hullot-Kentor, "What is Mechanical Reproduction?," 165), is capable of capturing artworks' trace rather than their aura, seeing commodity as it truly is, and reading the crowd and its city. Unfortunately, Paul is not a flâneur, though he may appear like one occasionally. Not possessing these capabilities, Paul ends up getting bewitched by art and commodity and experiencing the crowd in the wrong way. As a consequence, Paul pursues his dream so blindly that he has to kill himself in the end. Not only is Paul's 'un-flâneurie' environmentally fostered but also it is the root cause of his suicide.

NOTES

1. Janet Wolff argues that since women in the 19th century "could not stroll alone in the city," one must recognize that "the possibility of unmolested

strolling and observation first seen by Baudelaire, and then analyzed by Walter Benjamin were entirely the experiences of men". Of course, her viewpoint has been challenged by different critics. Here, the gendering of the flâneur is really not my concern. Therefore, I'll refer to the flâneur as "he" or "him" in this paper. See Janet Wolff, *Feminine Sentences: Essays on Women and Culture* (Cambridge: Polity, 1990) 41-58.

2. Most scholars, following Charles Baudelaire's depictions of a dandy in *The Painter of Modern Life and Other Essays,* have agreed that a dandy has evolved since the 19th century, and that a flâneur is like a dandy in the crowd. For instance, Priscilla Parkhurst Ferguson uses the term "the aristocratic ex-dandy". Bruce Mazlish is even more specific, "The passage to the flâneur and his modernity runs through the dandy on one side and the masses, or crowd, on the other. The dandy is a survival of the aristocratic principle…." See Priscilla Parkhurst Ferguson, "The Flâneur on and off the Streets of Paris," *The Flâneur,* ed. by Keith Tester (London: Routledge, 1994) 37, and Bruce Mazlish, "The Flâneur: From Spectator to Representation," *The Flâneur,* ed. by Keith Tester (London: Routledge, 1994) 49.
3. Nowadays, the Benjaminian aura has been invested with different conceptions. It can even be associated with computer technology. For instance, Richard Shief, in his "Digitized Analogies," states, "Digitization shows little respect for the integrity of objects, and so takes perception even further from the experience of aura." See Richard Shief, "Digitized Analogies," *Mapping Benjamin,* ed. by Hans Ulrich Gumbrecht and Michael Marrinan (Stanford: Stanford University Press, 2003) 69.
4. First, a flâneur normally has a very slow walking pace. In *Charles Baudelaire*, Benjamin states, "Around 1840…flâneurs liked to have the turtles set the pace for them." Above all, in the course of his slow stroll, a flâneur must have "great reminiscences, the historical shudder," or "dead facts—as something experienced and lived through". Plate states that a flâneur "must take up a Braille-like reading in which past time is made spatial in the present and offered to the senses to perceive." See Walter Benjamin, *Charles Baudelaire: A Lyric Poet in the Era of High Capitalism,* trans. by Harry Zohn (London: Verso, 1983) 54. Benjamin, *The Arcades Project,* M1.1 and M1.5, and Plate, 132.
5. Mazlish believes that a flâneur is "a poet, who observes daily, urban capitalist life…. He is the "dandy"…now forced to go on the market. He is the genius, whose spirit has been capitalized." Again, I must emphasize the sequentiality implied here: a true flâneur must observe "urban capitalist life" first before his spirit gets "capitalized". See Mazlish, 47

WORKS CITED

Arnold, Marilyn. *Willa Cather's Short Fiction.* Athens: Ohio University Press, 1984.

———. "Willa Cather." *Critical Survey of Short Fiction*, Volume 2. Ed Frank N. Magill. Pasadena: Salem Press, 1993. 450-56.

Baudelaire, Charles. *The Painter of Modern Life and Other Essays*. Ed. And trans. Jonathan Mayne. New York: Da Capo, 1986.

Benjamin, Walter. *Charles Baudelaire: A Lyric Poet in the Era of High Capitalism.* Trans. Harry Zohn. London: Verso, 1983.

———. *Illuminations.* Ed Hannah Arendt. Trans. Harry Zohn. Cambridge: Harvard University Press, 1992.

———. *The Arcades Project.* Trans. Howard Eiland and Kevin Mclaughlin. Cambridge: Belknap Press, 1999.

———. *Selected Writings, Volume 2, 1927-1943.* Ed. Michael W. Jennings, Howard Eiland, and Gary Smith. Cambridge: Belknap Press, 1999.

Brand, Dana. "From the Flâneur to the Detective: Interpreting the City of Poe." *Popular Fiction: Technology, Ideology, Production, Reading.* London: Routledge, 1990. 220-37.

Cather, Willa. "Paul's Case." *Willa Cather: Stories, Poems, and Other Writings.* Ed. Sharon O'Brien. New York: The Library of America, 1992. 468-88.

Cohen, Margaret. "Benjamin's Phantasmagoria: *The Arcades Project.*" *Walter Benjamin.* Ed. David S. Ferris. Cambridge: Cambridge University Press, 2004.

Crabtree, Sherry. "Cather's PAUL'S CASE." *Explicator*, Volume 58 Issue 4 (Summer 2000): 206-08.

Ferguson, Priscilla Parkhurst. "The Flâneur on and off the Streets of Paris." *The Flâneur*. Ed. Keith Tester. New York: Routledge, 1994. 22-42.

Frisby, David. "The Flâneur in Social Theory." *The Flâneur*. Ed. Keith Tester. New York: Routledge, 1994. 81-110.

Gilloch, Graeme. *Walter Benjamin: Critical Constellations.* Cambridge: Polity, 2002.

Hicks, Jennifer. "Paul's Case: Heredity or Environment?" *Short Stories for Students*, Volume 2. Ed. Kathleen Wilson. Detroit: Gale Research, 1997. 200-03.

Hullot-Kentor, Robert. "What Is Mechanical Reproduction?" *Mapping Benjamin.* Ed. Timothy Lenoir and Hans Ulrich Gumbrecht. Stanford: Stanford University Press, 2003. 158-71.

Koepnick, Lutz. *Walter Benjamin and the Aesthetics of Power.* Lincoln: University of Nebraska Press, 1999.

Lee, Hermoine. *Willa Cather: A Life Saved Up.* London: Virago, 1989.

Link-Heer, Ursula. "Aura Hysterica or the Lifted Gaze of the Object." *Mapping Benjamin.* Ed. Timothy Lenoir and Hans Ulrich Gumbrecht. Stanford: Stanford University Press, 2003. 114-24.

Mazlish, Bruce. "The Flâneur: From Spectator to Representation." *The Flâneur*. Ed. Keith Tester. New York: Routledge, 1994. 43-60.

Nardin, Jane. "Homosexual Identities in Willa Cather's "Paul Case"." *Literature and History*, Volume 17 No. 2 (October 2008): 31-46.

Nichols, Stephen G. "The End of Aura?" *Mapping Benjamin.* Ed. Timothy Lenoir and Hans Ulrich Gumbrecht. Stanford: Stanford University Press, 2003. 256-69.

O'Brien, Sharon. *Willa Cather: The Emerging Voice.* New York: Oxford University Press, 1987.

Page, Philip. "The Theatricality of Willa Cather's "Paul's Case"." *Studies in Short Fiction*, Volume 28 Issue 4 (Fall 1991): 553-57.

Pitcher, Edward W. "Willa Cather's "Paul's Case" and the Faustian Temperament." *Studies in Short Fiction*, Vol. 28 Issue 4 (Fall 1991): 543-52.

Plate, S. Brent. *Walter Benjamin, Religion, and Aesthetics.* New York: Routledge, 2005.

Randall, John H. *The Landscape and the Looking Glass.* Boston: Houghton, 1960.

Rosowski, Susan J. *The Voyage Perilous.* Lincoln: University of Nebraska Press, 1986.

Salda, Michael N. "What Really Happens in Cather's "Paul's Case"?" *Studies in Short Fiction*, Vol. 29 No. 1 (Winter 1992): 113-19.

Schmidt, Siegfried J. "From Aura-Loss to Cyberspace: *Further Thoughts on Walter Benjamin.*" *Mapping Benjamin.* Ed. Timothy Lenoir and Hans Ulrich Gumbrecht. Stanford: Stanford University Press, 2003. 63-71.

Shields, Rob. "Fancy Footwork: Walter Benjamin's notes on flâneurie." *The Flâneur*. Ed. Keith Tester. New York: Routledge, 1994. 61-80.

Shiff, Richard. "Digitized Analogies." *Mapping Benjamin.* Ed. Timothy Lenoir and Hans Ulrich Gumbrecht. Stanford: Stanford University Press, 2003. 63-71.

Tester, Keith. Introduction. *The Flâneur*. Ed. Tester. New York: Routledge, 1994. 1-21.

Wasserman, Loretta. "Is Cather's Paul a Case?" *Short Stories for Students Volume 2.* Ed. Kathleen Wilson. Detroit: Gale Research, 1997. 203-06.

White, Edmund. *The Flâneur*. New York: Bloomsbury Publishing, 2001.

Wilson, Kathleen, ed. *Short Stories for Students Volume 2.* Ed. Kathleen Wilson. Detroit: Gale Research, 1997.

Wolfarth, Irving. "The Measure of the Possible, the Weight of the Real and the Heat of the Moment: Benjamin's Actuality Today." *The Actuality of Walter Benjamin.* Ed. Laura Marcus and Lynday Nead. London: Lawrence and Wishart, 1998.

Wolff, Janet. *Feminine Sentences: Essays on Women and Culture.* Cambridge: Polity, 1990.

Different Planes of Consciousness in Sri Aurobindo's Later Sonnets

GOUTAM GHOSAL

SRI AUROBINDO'S later sonnets are like diary entries indicating his spiritual autobiography, his inner consciousness on the move from one state to another state, his multiple moods of realization. The chronological order prepared by the editors of the *Sonnets* (1999) is a bit confusing, because sometimes a sonnet placed earlier in the order is deeper in realization than a sonnet placed later in the sequence. In my brief paper, I shall try to show how Sri Aurobindo projects cosmic consciousness in certain lines and then goes beyond to a deeper realization in some other lines. According to Sri Aurobindo, the psychic being is our true self, the inmost being and his yoga begins when this being comes to the front and takes the lead of our being. This initiates a great widening of our consciousness and helps us to identify ourselves with the whole world. In "The Indwelling Universal", Sri Aurobindo projects his cosmic awareness in the very first line—"I contain the wide world in my soul's embrace". The whole of the second quatrain speaks of this awareness in detail.

> All eyes that look on me are my sole eyes;
> The one heart that beats within all breasts is mine.
> The world's happiness flows through me like wine,
> Its million sorrows are my agonies (*Sonnets*: 19: 1999)

The next sonnet is entitled "Bliss of Identity". This goes beyond cosmic consciousness. Here the identification is directly with the Divine after it starts from cosmic awareness in the first quatrain with an expressive line "All beings are in myself embraced" (20). From cosmic consciousness Sri Aurobindo smoothly passes into the Knowledge by Identity, a feeling of oneness with the Supreme Being.

> Thy spirit's infinite breath I feel in me;
> My life is a throb of Thy eternity. (20)

The Knowledge by Identity is sometimes initiated by the descent of the Golden or the supramental Light in a progressive manner beginning from the brain, throat and heart and finally enveloping the feet of the poet after which he sees the earth as the Divine's playfield and His seat (28). The identification seems complete in certain sonnets. Certain lines in "Omnipresence" are curious. You have either to believe them or reject them as poetic rubbish. The lines are bare. Here is my selection:

He is in me, round me, facing everywhere. (60)
He has become my substance and my breath. (60)

The sonnet entitled "Immortality" shows once again the kind of identity the poet has established with the Supreme Being.

I have drunk deep of God's own liberty
From which an occult sovereignty derives:
Hidden in an earthly garment that survives,
I am the worldless being vast and free.
A moment stamped with that supremacy
Has rescued me from cosmic looks and gyves;
Abolishing death and time my nature lives
In the deep heart of immortality. (61)

These are some instances when Sri Aurobindo goes beyond cosmic consciousness to reveal his experiences of identity with the Supreme Divine.

But then, what are the sources of his spiritual sonnets speaking of his identity with the Divine? To answer this question we must try to go by Sri Aurobindo's own theory of overhead poetics. Sri Aurobindo tells us that the psychic is not a spiritual plane proper and that it is a gateway to the spiritual planes (Sethna: 7: 1972). The spiritual or the overhead planes are the Higher mind, the Illumined mind, the Intuition and the Overmind. The overmind is the last summit of the mind. It is a gateway to the supermind, which is Sri Aurobindo's brand name of a new species beyond the territory of mental man. The supermind or the supramental is yet to be expressed in language. But, something of the supermind principles and characteristics flows down to the overmind. The *mantra* or mantric poetry or the poetry of incantation is created by the touch of the overmind or very high intuition. The *mantra* is a revelatory speech, the supremely inevitable utterance. It is the poetry of vision, revelation, incantation, prayer and magic. But how can we know what plane of consciousness is touching which line in a poem? Sri

Aurobindo has clarified the characteristics of the planes leaving for us the task of recognizing which plane is affecting which line in a poem. "I mean by the Higher Mind a first plane of spiritual consciousness where one becomes constantly and closely aware of the Self..." (*SABCL* 9: 342). Elsewhere, in *The Life Divine*, Sri Aurobindo is more specific about its nature when he says, "...but its special character, its activity of consciousness are dominated by Thought" (*SABCL* 19: 939). It may be a luminous zone, but the stress is on very high thought, which we mostly see in the poetry of Milton. The following aphorism from "The Call of the Impossible" indicates higher spiritual thought:

What shines above, waits darkling here in us. (*Sonnets*: 8)

The next stage up in the consciousness is the Illumined Mind. Sri Aurobindo explains: "A greater Force [than the Higher Mind] is that of the illumined Mind, a Mind no longer of higher thought, but of spiritual light" (*SABCL* 19: 944). Sri Aurobindo observes its characteristics in detail.

Here the clarity of spiritual intelligence, its tranquil daylight, gives place or subordinates itself to an intense lustre, a splendour and illumination of the spirit: a play of lightnings of spiritual truth and power breaks from above into the consciousness and adds to the calm and wide enlightenment and the vast descent of peace which characterize or accompany the action of the larger conceptual-spiritual principle, a fiery ardour of realization and a rapturous ecstasy of knowledge. A downpour of inwardly visible light very usually envelops this action (944).

Talking of the Illumined Mind Sri Aurobindo usually highlights a kind of brilliant spiritual lights and colours pressed into the front with what he calls "rapturous ecstasy of knowledge". In a sonnet entitled "Evolution", Sri Aurobindo seems to be drawing his inspiration from the illumined Mind in the following lines:

Mind liberated swam Light's ocean vast,
And life escaped from its grey tortured line;
I saw Matter illumining its parent Night.
The soul could feel into infinity cast
Timeless God-bliss the heart incarnadine. (7)

The Higher Mind and the Illumined Mind are surpassed by a third level of consciousness, which Sri Aurobindo calls the Intuition. Sri Aurobindo explains in *The Life Divine*: "Intuition is a power of consciousness nearer and more intimate to the original Knowledge by Identity; for it is always something that leaps out direct from a concealed identity" (*SABCL* 19: 946). The sonnet entitled "Now I Have Borne" begins with a flash of Intuition:

> Now I have borne Thy presence and Thy light,
> Eternity assumes me and I am
> A vastness of tranquillity and flame... (*Sonnets*: 17)

Intuition is very close to the overmind and therefore quite often the supermind knowledge secretly creeps in the messages of Intuition. The overmind is a kind of delegation from the supermind. Sri Aurobindo explains in a letter:

> The overmind sees calmly, steadily, in great masses and large extensions of space and time and relation, globally; it creates and acts in the same way—it is the world of the great Gods, the divine creators. (*SABCL* 24: 1154)

Poetry or lines that come from the overmind are supremely revelatory and inevitable utterances. Such lines cannot be improved upon. These are mantric or incantatory lines, which are rare even in the world's greatest poetry. While such lines are more frequent in Sri Aurobindo's cosmic epic, *Savitri*, even in the sonnets, there are lines like that, which go beyond all analysis. They come from the Infinite and disappear into the Infinite.

> A momentless intensity pure and bare,
> I stretch to an eternal everywhere. (*Sonnets*: 39)

> I have looked, alive, upon the Eternal's face. (51)

> I shall be merged in the Lonely and Unique
> And wake into a sudden blaze of God,
> The marvel and rapture of the Apocalypse. (29)

Sri Aurobindo explains in a letter to K.D. Sethna:

> The overmind is essentially a spiritual power. Mind in it surpasses its ordinary self and rises and takes its stand on a spiritual foundation. It embraces beauty and sublimates it; it has an essential aesthesis which is not limited by rules and canons; it sees a universal and an eternal beauty while it takes up an transforms all that is limited and particular. (Sethna: 50)

Something of the Supermind percolates down into the overmind. The sonnets touch all the overhead planes starting from the Higher mind, the Illumined Mind and the Intuition and ranging upto the overmind. As the overmind is also the source of cosmic consciousness, it is easy to see how Sri Aurobindo's lines in the sonnets express that plane of mind, which is the gateway to the Supermind. Another letter from Sri Aurobindo to Sethna sheds more light on the plane and the obvious influence of that source on the sonnets:

> The Overmind is not strictly a transcendental consciousness—that epithet would more accurately apply to the Supramental and to the Sachchidananda consciousness—though it looks up to the transcendental and may receive something from it and though it does transcend the ordinary human mind and, in its full and native self-power when it does not lean down and become part of mind, is superconscient to us. It is more properly a cosmic consciousness, even the very base of the cosmic as we perceive, understand or feel it. It stands behind every particular in the cosmos and is the source of all our mental, vital or physical actualities and possibilities which are diminished and degraded derivations and variations from it and have not, except in certain formations and activities of genius and some intense self-exceeding, anything of the native overmind quality and power. Nevertheless, because it stands behind as if covered by a veil, something of it can break through or shine through or even dimly glimmer through and that brings the overmind touch or note. (Sethna: 13-14)

The passage cited above clearly indicates the various types of overmind influence on poetry, sometimes a flickering touch or hazy influence or the sudden direct transmission. However, in Sri Aurobindo's sonnets, the cosmic self creeps in too often with a suggestion of the Infinite both on the substance and on the style. The sonnet form had been used by Petrarch and Shakespeare to express either their mundane tension or their intense love mounting up to a cosmic dimension. Sri Aurobindo uses the form to indicate how the new poets can utilize the form to communicate their cosmic realizations, how it can record the route map to the highest, how it can image the feelings of cosmic consciousness and Oneness. The Supermind is yet unexpressed and at this stage of spiritual evolution can only express itself, to some extent, through the Overmind. Sri Aurobindo has tried to give a new dimension to the sonnet form by introducing a new substance for it.

Sri Aurobindo did not use the form as a mere literary exercise. He wished to experiment if his yogic experience, which was a subjective experience, could be communicated in various forms of the traditional sonnet. Very interestingly, he uses the Shakespearean form to indicate the descent of the Supramental light on the human body in "The Golden Light".

Thy golden Light came down into my brain
And the grey rooms of mind sun-touched became
A bright reply to Wisdom's occult plane,
A calm illumination and a flame.

Thy golden Light came down into my throat,
And all my speech is now a tune divine,
A paen song of Thee my single note;
My words are drunk with the Immortal's wine.

Thy golden Light came down into my heart
Smiting my life with Thy eternity;
Now has it grown a temple where Thou art
And all its passions point towards only Thee.

Thy golden Light came down into my feet;
My earth is now Thy playfield and Thy seat. (*Sonnets*: 29)

The gradually descending Light is recorded in bare images. Unlike mystic poetry, which may contain much of the decorative stuff as we see in *Gitanjali,* the spiritual poetry proper is bare, a direct vision of Truth, a clear direct experience. This poetry transcribes Truth's own language, as the Upanishadic poets did. It is not always attractive and raises the question of "Objective Correlative". But then, the question also leads us to the question: who was Sri Aurobindo's target audience? He always claimed that his early poetry was not received in a changed aesthetic weather and that his later poetry belonged to the future, meaning thereby a change of consciousness in the future humanity. Let us come back to his interesting sonnet in the Shakespearean form. In Sri Aurobindo's yoga, there is an ascent of consciousness and there is also a descent of consciousness. It is often simultaneous. The seer-poet is here speaking of the Supramental descent in a gradual course, starting from the brain, then to the throat, then to the heart-centre and finally to the feet indicating the climax of the process. The couplet is reserved for the peak of experience, as a conclusive note here. There is yet much to be said about the Light, but that is not possible within the brief compact structure of a sonnet. Sri Aurobindo's philosophy implies not just an ascent into the Light, but also the Light's eagerness to descend into the gross physical, the material life.

> This descent is felt as a pouring in of calm and peace, of force and power, of light, of joy and ecstasy, of wideness and freedom and knowledge, of a Divine Being or a Presence—sometimes one of these, sometimes several of them or all together. (Sri Aurobindo: *SABCL*, vol. 23: 991-92)

Each quartrain speaks of the reaction too, the change of consciousness initiated by the golden Light. The immediate response is an answer of acceptance. The human speech is transformed in the second quartrain. Sri Aurobindo is helpless with words. He has to choose the vocabulary from the Upanishads: hence "Immortal's wine". What other language can one use to express the "Immortal", or the "Deathless" or "Luminous" to express such an experience? The response and acceptance from the heart-centre is extremely important in Sri Aurobindo's yoga; hence the feeling of eternity. Finally, the Divine light descends on the earth-nature and occupies it.

Unlike the lyric poetry of Sri Aurobindo or even *Savitri*, the sonnets are not quite attractive to the common human intelligence. They are often snapshots of a day's experience or a week's or a month's experience. They may be called records of yoga in a very sophisticated form.

WORKS CITED

Aurobindo, Sri. *Sonnets*, Pondicherry: Sri Aurobindo Ashram Publication Department, 1980, 1999.

———. *Sri Aurobindo Birth Centenary Library*, Volume 9, Pondicherry: Sri Aurobindo Ashram, 1972.

———. *SABCL*, Volume 19, Pondicherry: Sri Aurobindo Ashram, 1970.

———. *SABCL*, Volume 23 (Letters on Yoga), Pondicherry: Sri Aurobindo Ashram, 1970.

Sethna, K.D. *Overhead Poetry: Poems with Sri Aurobindo's Comments*, Pondicherry: Sri Aurobindo International Centre of Education, 1972.

Bakhtin's Metaphor of Carnival: An Epiphanic Reassessment of Ananthamurthy's *Samskara*

ANITA MYLES

MIKHAIL BAKHTIN (1895-1975), the Russian philosopher and literary theorist employed the terms carnival, carnivalisation and carnivalesque with the view to denote the use and significance of carnivals in works of literature. He described carnivals as 'a literary mode that subverts and liberates the assumption of the dominant style and atmosphere through humour and chaos'. In two of his works, *The Problems of Dostoevsky's Poetics* (1929) and *Rabelais and His World* (1965) Bakhtin states that the carnivalesque in literature often subscribes to those activities that take place in carnivals of popular culture claiming that in carnivals the suppressed voices are heard a loud with a sense of liberation from any sort of authority.

Bakhtin stipulated four categories of the carnivalistic sense of the world:

1. **Familiar and free interaction between people:** carnival encouraged the getting together of people of varied hierarchies, interaction and freedom of expression. In this way the artificial boundaries created by social norms were forgotten for some time.

2. **Eccentric behaviour:** once again the restrictions on behaviour were waved off and the natural self was given ample opportunity to express itself.

3. **Carnivalistic misalliance:** this implicated that the most contradictory alliances which were normally disallowed were permitted to unite without any inhibitions and fear of exposure to the public eye.

4. **Sacrilegious:** Bakhtin opined that sacrilegious events were permitted to take place without the fear of punishment. According to the critic such activities were mere 'theatrical expressions of manifested life experiences' taking the form of 'sensual ritualistic performances'.

Bakhtin proffered literary forms which include descriptions of carnivals actually demonstrate a resistance to authority. Carnivals substantiate cultural changes and interactions without the intervention of authorities. They denote a 'polyphonic' note to the piece of literature that includes carnivals thereby granting freedom of expression to characters encouraging them to explicate themselves subversively and also shockingly. Thus the carnival creates a moment when everything is permissible, a situation in which diverse voices are heard, breaking traditions and enabling genuine dialogue. Bakhtin traces the significance of the carnival to the ancient times when such activities created alternate social space, strongly tinged with freedom, equality and abundance. Undoubtedly, human relationships assume a new meaning on such occasions as individual tendencies are overshadowed by the collective. During the carnival the individual experiences freedom to its utmost where the defining feature definitely amounts to festivity with the demolition of all social barriers. In such situations pleasures of the body become prime emphasizing on the sensual and the senses.

Literary and social historians Peter Stallybrass and Allen White aptly observed:

> Carnival in its widest, most general sense embraced ritual spectacles such as fairs, popular feasts and wakes, processions and competitions...comic shows, mummery and dancing, open-air amusements with costumes, masks, giants, dwarfs, monsters, trained animals and so forth; it included comic verbal compositions...such as parodies, travesties, and vulgar farce; and it included curses, oaths, slang, humour, popular tricks and jokes, scatological forms, in fact all the "low" and "dirty" sorts of folk humour. Carnival is presented by Bakhtin as a world of topsy-turvy, of heteroglot exuberance, of ceaseless over running and excess where all is mixed, hybrid, ritually degraded and defiled. (8)

Further, P. Deloria proclaimed that according to Bakhtin:

> [Carnival] represented a second life, a different consciousness that transcended the everyday. In the festive practices of the common people of Europe [Bakhtin] saw a topsy-turvy, mocking way of being that questioned the rationalized administrative power of the state. As both specific holiday ritual and generalized consciousness, carnival broke down boundaries, demonstrating the commonalities between upper and lower classes, law and custom, food and flesh, past and present, civilized and savage, birth and death. It replaced all forms of rank and hierarchy with boundless utopian freedom. Over time,

> the impact of these different consciousnesses may painstakingly transform the larger structures of society. (15-16)

R. Stam conclusively stated:

> Carnival for Bakhtin refers to the pre-Lenten revelry whose origins can be traced back to the Dionysian festivities of the Greeks and Saturnalia of the Romans, but which enjoyed its apogee of both observance and symbolic meaning in the High Middle Ages. In that period, Bakhtin points out, carnival represented an alternative cosmovision characterized by the ludic undermining of all norms. The carnivalesque principle abolishes hierarchies, levels social classes, and creates another life free from conventional rules and restrictions. In carnival all that is marginalized and excluded—the mad, the scandalous, the oleatory—takes over the centre in a liberating explosion of otherness. (86)

The preceding citations reiterate the stance that Bakhtin's concept of carnival was a complicated and dynamic social and cultural practice. At the same time Bakhtin found carnival to be interesting not just because of what it was but also because of what it did—its social functions. Bakhtin emphasized the liberating and subversive potentiality of the carnival. Subscribing to this view, Terry Eagleton remarked,

> Carnival after all is a licensed affair. In every sense, a permissible rupture of hegemony, a contained popular blow off as disturbing and relatively in effectual as a revolutionary work of art. (148)

Bakhtin observed that carnival and folk culture were on the decline since the eighteenth century. However, in Indian literature in translation the portrayal of carnivals along with its inherent significance as stipulated in all the four categories of the carnivalistic sense of the world by Bakhtin is fully evident. This paper intends to apply Bakhtin's theory to U.R. Ananthamurthy's well known work *Samskara.*

The latter half of the novel narrates how in a state of indecisiveness over the performing of the last rites of Narranappa Praneshacharya walks towards the forest. While returning back to the agarhara he is accosted by Chandri the low caste concubine of Narranappa pleading with the Acharya to cremate the dead body of Narranappa. While she falls on his feet seeking his blessings, the warm touch of Chandri arouses sensual instincts in Praneshacharya who is overcome by his emotions and has a physical relationship with her. His guilt surmounts to an extent that now he is neither able to confess his sin nor guide the people of the agarhara as their spiritual leader. On returning home he finds that his wife Bhagirathi was afflicated with plague and she soon dies.

After performing the last rites of Bhagirathi, Praneshacharya hurriedly walks away from Durvasapura heading towards Kundapura. His mind is continuously hounded by a flutter of thoughts, some rational others irrational. He ruminates on his marriage with the invalid Bhagirathi. Ananthamurthy describes the situation in the following words:

> When he married her he was sixteen, she twelve. He had thought he should renounce the world, become a sanyasi, live a life of self-sacrifice. That was the ideal, the challenge of his boyhood days. So he had married a born invalid deliberately. He'd left her in the grateful house of her father, gone to Benares, studied to become "the Crest-Jewel of Vedanta Philosophy", and had come back. Here was the Lord's ordeal for him, waiting, to test him whether he had the strength to live and act by non-attachment—that was why He had given an ailing invalid wife into his hands. He would serve her, delighting in that knowledge. He had cooked for her, fed her the wheat-gruel he had himself made, done meticulously every act of daily worship for the gods, read and explicated the holy texts for the Brahmins—Ramayana, Bharata, Bhagwata, etc.—hoarded his penances like a miser his money. (66)

Continuing to walk deeply engrossed in thought he is pursued by Putta, the Riddleman who spots him going and hastily begins to follow him till he catches up. Putta puts forth a torrent of questions thus quizzing Praneshacharya most probably attempting to extricate some dark inner-most secret from him. Pursuing him further on Putta leads Praneshacharya to the bustle of the temple-car festival at Melige. Ananthamurthy describes the carnival in minute detail picturising both the colour and the mood that overshadowed the place.

Putta led Praneshacharya to a shop where they bought coconuts and bananas to offer at the temple there. However, before enqueuing at the temple they decide to look around. For Praneshacharya the sight is enticing while Putta enjoys each moment to the core. Vivid descriptions of children moving around with reed pipes, smells of burning camphor and joss sticks, the smell of new clothes accompanied by the song of the balloon seller enliven the atmosphere. While Putta engages himself in some entertainment at the Bombay Box Praneshacharya stealthily tries to escape his company, but Putta is too cunning for him. Then

Putta leads him to the site of the acrobatic show where a 'shapely serpentine woman' balanced herself 'on her bare belly at the end of a bamboo pole'. The crowd threw copper coins at the girl. While Putta was engrossed in the activities at the fair Praneshacharya 'felt like a hovering demon, a rootless object in the hustle and noise' (98). He was not at peace with himself as his mind was still in a state of flux due to his leaving the village all of a sudden with no particular destination whatsoever in mind. Putta continued to have his way at the carnival while 'Praneshacharya stood outside this world of ordinary pleasures and looked at the gathered crowd' pondering—'the whole thing was a matter of expectation, experience, contentment' (98). Praneshacharya was absolutely entranced in this world of untold pleasures and frequently thought of Chandri '[hers] too is the same world. But I am neither here nor there. I am caught in the play of opposites' (99). Narranappa was perhaps bolder to have relinquished his world of astute Brahmanism to enjoy the pleasures of Chandri's realm. As Putta leads him on to witness the cock fight Praneshacharya is panic stricken abruptly dropping into a rather demonic world. The world that he saw would make a Brahmin like him wilt instantly.

As he watched the violent cockfight:

> It became clear that he did not have the skill to live in this world of sharp and cruel feelings. One part of lust is tenderness, the other part a demoniac will. Cowardice returned, the cowardice he had felt the day Narranappa had defied him, when the whole person seemed to shrink before that arrogance. (100)

Putta was in a different world altogether, elated beyond limits for betting in the cockfight especially as he won twelve annas. Praneshacharya tried his utmost to extricate himself from the forced company of Putta but unfortunately 'The man's sympathies were like creepers that tangle your feet' (101). Praneshacharya continues to learn another lesson about life from Putta. He watches Putta bargain with the goldsmith while attempting to sell the gold ring that Praneshacharya possessed. He realized soon that 'in this iron age of *Kali*, you can't be that dumb and survive' (102). Putta then takes him to the house of the whore Padmavati promising to bring Praneshacharya back to her house after he has had his meal at the temple. However, Praneshacharya skillfully avoided meeting Padmavati and proceeded towards Durvasapura in a cart that was passing by. He had already begun to miss the company of Putta. His mind was in a state of upheaval as to what he would do without Putta "Praneshacharya waited; anxious, expectant" (118).

The questions that arise in the mind of Praneshacharya lead him into new and ordinary worlds that he has just experienced in the company of Putta simultaneously realizing that so long he was unaware of life beyond his books and his duties as a Brahmin Pundit of the agarhara. He has had the privilege to get acquainted with the worlds of both Narranappa as well as of Putta. As Putta takes him on a tour through the temple festival and fair also to the whorehouse and the pawnshop Praneshacharya is introduced to a new world of passion and sensation hitherto unknown to him.

The description of the carnival in *Samskara* is epiphanic in nature. Gradually a change appears in the thought pattern of Praneshacharya. Though he was a mute spectator to the activities at the fair yet there is an intense inner urge to ascertain his personal identity. There is a need to liberate him from the rigid almost dehumanizing code of religious customs that he had practiced for so long. Putta paves the way for the Acharya by guiding him through the sensuous and sensual experiences of life about which he was not cognizant so far. Praneshacharya almost begins to envy Putta who easily accommodates to situations in life. Putta readily accepts his own ambiguous caste status. He is permitted to wear the scared thread but he cannot eat with the Brahmins. At the fair he becomes a part of it enjoying to the core the noise, the smells and the visual delights. Praneshacharya was constantly gripped with the fear of being recognized at the fair and even at the temple while dinning with the other Brahmins.

A.K. Ramanujan, the translator of the novel *Samskara* emphasizes that the novel is structured like a *Samskara* for it has three stages of (1) separation, (2) transition, and (3) reincorporation. These three stages are apparent in the life of Praneshacharya. He goes away from the agarhara which is separation, the first stage. Then he travels through the forest, has an encounter with Chandri, meets Putta and goes to the fair which brings about a new orientation in him leading to the second stage of transition. Finally the third stage comes when he moves towards re-incorporation after realizing that life does not mean asceticism alone, it not only has a spiritual side to it but also a physical side. Significantly enough this is the moment of epiphany, of challenges and changes. All the battles of tradition and its defiance, of asceticism versus sensuality, of meaning and meaninglessness of ritual, of desire versus salvation have now become a part and parcel of Praneshacharya. Gradually the venue of the novel has shifted from the Hindu village community to the body and spirit of Praneshacharya, the protagonist. His journey and his experience at the carnival change his perspective of life completely and force him to envision life in a new light. His life so far has been one of challenges and changes. There are immense psychological upheavals within Praneshacharya. Putta appears to be his alter ego manifesting blatantly those aspects of life which he had missed and more relevantly consciously avoided as an astute ascetic.

Samskara may be symbolically and appropriately interpreted on the basis of the four categories of carnivalistic doctrine of Bakhtin. Primarily Bakhtin stipulated a familiar and free interaction between masses emphasizing that during a carnival people of varied hierarchies, interact with ample freedom of expression. In this way the artificial boundaries created by social norms were forgotten for some time. There is a free interaction between Putta, the half caste and Praneshacharya, the respected Brahmin. While Putta enjoyed the freedom of speech Praneshacharya was gripped with numerous untold fears. Putta narrates his ancestry of being the son of a high class Brahmin and a low class woman to Praneshacharya. He had gone through the sacred thread ceremony but he preferred to be recognized as a low class man for he enjoyed greater freedom of behaviour this way. He takes the liberty to describe his married life to Praneshacharya confiding that he had two children and his wife belonged to Kundapura. He continues to say that his wife insisted on going to her father's house at least once a month resulting in quarrels between Putta and his wife who even resorted to beating her for her adamancy. He expected the Acharya to comment on his wife but he only laughed and so did Putta. Strangely enough Praneshacharya for once does not feel that he was in the company of a half breed who were shunned by high-class Brahmins. Praneshacharya took the liberty to eat whatever was offered by Putta. In the temple festival too, people of all castes were allowed to mingle together because the mood of the carnival temporarily dismantled the traditional wall of caste and creed.

The second hypothesis of Bakhtin claims that the restrictions on behavior were waved off and the natural self was given ample opportunity to express itself. As described in the novel while enjoying and participating in multiple amusements of the carnival the intermixing and tabooed free conversation creates an atmosphere of social equality and an awareness that each member of the crowd was a part of the larger humanity. In this way the carnival definitely has a cathartic function for society. People waited for the whole year to participate in the temple chariot festival. They forgot their day to day worries by participating in the temple festivities and were awestruck by the colourful wares displayed for both the young and the old. Bakhtin's idea of the most contradictory alliances which were normally disallowed were permitted to unite without any inhibitions and fear of exposure to the public eye during a carnival find ample evidence in the novel *Samskara.*

In the fourth but the most significant part of the theory Bakhtin opined that sacrilegious events were allowed to take place without the fear of punishment. According to the critic such activities were mere 'theatrical expressions of manifested life experiences' taking the form of 'sensual ritualistic performances'. Praneshacharya and Putta watch the cock fight on the hillock nearby; Putta enjoys each and every maneuver while Praneshacharya stands aloof a little upset by the violence involved. While Putta is engrossed in betting Praneshacharya becomes impatient and gradually moves away from the place. Similarly the acrobatic show performed by a curvaceous young acrobat gypsy girl "swinging in her exercises in the sky at the end of the bamboo pole, wearing body tight clothes" (103) fascinates Putta. He then takes Praneshacharya to the house of a female acquaintance Padmavati who was known for her seductive charms. Putta has no inhibitions in introducing the Acharya to Padmavati. Thus Putta initiated Praneshacharya into a world of sensuous and sensual experiences making Praneshacharya comment "I dread it. It's the dread of being transformed from ghost to demon" (103). Ananthamurthy vividly describes the situation thus:

> So far he didn't even live; doing only what was done, chanting the same old mantra, he had remained inexperienced. Experience is risk, assault. A thing not done before, a joining in the dark of the jungle. He's thought experience was fulfillment of what one wanted, but now it seemed it was the unseen, the unpredicted, thrust into our life like breasts, entering it. (72)

Praneshacharya's encounter at this stage is an example of existentialist dilemma between physical allurement and spiritual cognizance. In spite of the seductive charm of the lady he succeeds in putting aside both desire and value. This part is epiphanic in nature because it brings before us a theological truth that spirituality becomes meaningful only after one succeeds in overcoming the temptations of the world. This is exactly what Bakhtin meant by carnivalistic purgation. The progression of life is meaningful only when we become conscious of our faults and overcome it the first possible opportunity. After getting seduced by Chandri, Praneshacharya was fully burdened by a guilt of sin but the company of Putta and his different encounters in the carnival help him to evolve.

WORKS CITED

Ananthamurthy, U.R. *Smaskara, A Rite for a Dead Man*. New Delhi: Oxford University Press, 2012 (second edition).

Bakhtin, M. *Rabelais and His World* (Helene Iswolsky, Trans.), Indiana University Press, 2009 edition.

———. *Problems of Dostoevsky's Poetics* (C. Emerson, Trans.), Minneapolis: University of Minnesota Press, 1984.

Deloria, P. *Playing Indian*. New Haven, CT: Yale University Press, 1998.

Eagleton, T. *Walter Benjamin or Towards a Revolutionary Criticism*. London: Verso, 1981.

Stallybrass, P. and White, A. *The Politics and Poetics of Transgression*. Ithaca, NY: Cornell University Press, 1986.

Stam, R. *Subversive Pleasures: Bakhtin Cultural Criticism and Film*. Baltimore, MD: John Hopkins University Press, 1989.

"Boomerang and a Cricket Bat": Rethinking the White Nation's Civilizing Mission

ARINDAM DAS

OTHER than in certain disperse studies (such as Ronald Hyam's *Britain's Imperial Century, 1815-1914: A Study of Empire and Expansion* (1976)) one of the comparatively neglected agencies in the transfer of culture from the center of settler colony to its margin subjects is sports and games. Sports, games and its related fields are definitely ideological constructs that propagate state agendas through organized authorities such as clubs, formalized games department and related institutes. As a colonial ideological apparatus sports authorities canonized certain white games excluding other indigenous ones. This compelled the marginalized not merely to gradually adopt hitherto unknown games and their parameters but even compete with the whites in these games—an affair that may not be dismissed as too simplistic and easy from the Indigenous vantage point. Further, percolation of a colonial sport amongst the Indigenous colonized masses sets the frame for the further analysis of the same within the elaboration of colonial civilizing zeal and modern paternalistic culture of "Enlightenment". My article shall elaborate the same by taking up as a case study the Aboriginal cricket team's visit to England in 1867-68.

But, before we proceed further a theoretical frame for the better understanding of the same is imperative. The very concept of sports as a part of cultural power may be set in the wider context of the theoretical literature in the works of Antonio Gramsci. Gramsci's hegemony operates within the presence of a duality: force/consent and violence/persuasion. And, it is this that characterizes the power calculas. Gramsian hegemony is a consensual alliance or association of groups that have same interest; and where one particular group leads the other. However, if a group leads the allied group (through a matter of consent) then it dominates the antagonistic group (through a form of force). Hence, hegemony is a straddling and even a balancing between force and consent, where force is not led to prevail over consent. An economy of violence is maintained and this points to the methods by which force, coercion, and violence are limited and circumscribed, and highlights the ways and means by which moral, intellectual, and ideological belief systems are implicated in the attaining and maintaining of power structures. When consent and consequent leadership of one group over another come to play, then the consenting group that enters into an alliance/coalition needs to transcend narrow vested interests of race, nation, class and social groups to adopt a more universal worldview. This leads one to understand as to how hegemony generates and organizes the mechanics and dynamics of knowledge/ideology/belief system production and dissemination. Hence, hegemony is at once political and cultural—dominating and pedagogic. Moreover, hegemony first is applied within a group that leads to a formation of an entity possessing the capacity to rule; and then beyond the group over other groups (political or cultural or both) to disseminate the superior group's worldview.

Gramsci's concept of cultural hegemony had been employed by theorists like Richard Gruneau (*Class, Sports, and Social Development*) and Jennifer Hargreaves (*Sports, Culture, and Ideology*) to investigate the social developments in sports under exploitative frame. Sports theorists like Huizinga (1955), Schmitz (1988), Novak (1976) and Guttmann (1978) claim that games, sports and plays are voluntary activities autonomous of any material or other instrumental forms. Suspending the fact that play and games admit any form of compulsion or obligation associated with material survival, Huizinga observes about play as:

> …a free activity standing quite consciously outside "ordinary" life as being "not serious", but at the same time absorbing the player intensely and utterly. It is an activity connected with no material interest, and no profit can be gained by it. It proceeds within its own proper boundaries of time and space according to fixed rules and in an orderly manner. It promotes the formation of social groupings which tends to surround themselves with secrecy and to stress their difference from the common world by disguise or other means. (13)

In no different vein Schmitz formulates the basic tenets of play:

> …play seems to begin by abandoning forms of everyday behaviour, but it maintains that abandonment in a positive and determinate way by creating a new space and time with new forms and rules of behaviour that are not determined by or functional within the everyday world but which nevertheless have a positive meaning

> of their own. Within its boundaries and objectives the play-world exhibits a totality of meaning and value that is strikingly complete and perfect. Play reveals itself as transnatural, limited perfection. (33)

Critiquing such a liberalist stance that tends to separate sports and play from State and politics, Gruneau divulges the reason behind such facile assumptions:

> (such theorists) ignore or underplay the significance of material history as a part of the constituting processes of the intentions of players, and of the rules, traditions, beliefs, and organizations which define play, game, and sporting activities at different historical moments. (50)

Thus as for Gruneau, even Hargreaves points to the exploitative and ideologically determined promotion of play and sports by the State: "ruling group attempt to use sport as an instrument of control" (42). Rightly does Jean-Marie Brohm point sport as an ideological state apparatus instrumental for reproducing the social relations of capitalism:

> Sport is an ideological State apparatus which fulfils a triple: ideologically reproduces bourgeois social relations such as selection and hierarchy, subservience, obedience, etc.; secondly, it spreads an organizational ideology specific to the institution of sport, involving competition, records and output; and thirdly, it transmits on a huge scale the general themes of ruling bourgeois ideology like the myth of superman, individualism, social advancement, success, efficiency etc. (77)

It is thereby this hegemonic tendency to culturally control and assimilate the colonized masses through the ideology of sports that is made evident in the Australian settler colony's "Enlightenment" zeal towards the native. This "Enlightenment" motive was an integral part of the modernist discourse of nation building of the white colonizers of Australia who tended to formulate a standard rubric for its subjects. Ernest Gellner in his *Nations and Nationalism* observes:

> ...when general social conditions make for standardised, homogeneous, centrally sustained high cultures, pervading entire populations and not just elite minorities, a situation arises in which well-defined educationally sanctioned and unified cultures constitute very nearly the only kind of unit with which men willingly identify. The cultures now seem to be the natural repositories of political legitimacy. (55)

Nationalism for Gellner is an outcome of affiliation to a Puritanistic "High" culture of the secular intelligentsia and a dispensing with Pluralistic "Low" culture of unurbanized localities and folk communities. Nationalism thus leads inevitably to the oblivion of folk traditions and generates a social cohesion at the behest of modernity. Cricket in the colonized Australia formed a part of this high culture which was meant for the colonized masses to subscribe to. The neo-Marxist Gellner's concept of a "unified culture(s)" to which the subjects "willingly identify" takes its cue from Gramsci's "hegemony".

What might appear intriguing is that the first Australian team to tour England was not a White one but a group of Aboriginal men of Madi Madi and Wotjbaluk tribe from the Western District of Victoria. The list revealed a set of bizarre names—Dick-a-Dick, Tiger, Mosquito, Cuzens, Red Cap, Sundown, Twopenny, Jim Crow, Peter, Mullagh, Bullocky. When they played the M.C.C. at the famous Lord's ground they were opposed by an earl, a viscount, a lieutenant-colonel and a captain. Even the great W.G. Grace acknowledged they "acquitted themselves very well". The team's journey to England is recounted in D.J. Mulvaney's *Cricket Walkabouts: The Australian Aboriginal Cricketers on Tour 1867-68* (1967):

> Bullocky's bizarre pilgrimage to Lord's began on 16 September 1867 when with twelve Aboriginal team-mates, cook, coachman, English captain and Australian manager, he rolled out of the western Victorian hamlet of Edenhope, in a large American wagon drawn by four horses, supplied with tents and "tucker". That night their wagon bogged on the track. However, even the continuous rain during their eight-day trek to the coast at Warrnambool, under 150 miles distant, failed to dampen the team spirit for nocturnal hunting forays after possum and kangaroo. Charles Lawrence, their 'new chum' captain and coach, cheerfully adapted himself to the conditions and joined the hunters.
>
> The team made an auspicious entry onto the field to open its Victorian tour. At Warrnambool it scored 140, and then twice dismissed the sixteen-man European side in a total of 43 minutes. Their exit from the colony was even more auspicious. They proceeded in leisurely fashion from Warrnambool to Geelong, playing cricket at Mortlake en route. After the second of their two Geelong matches against the Corlo Club, and before supposedly resuming their Victorian tour, they

> drove to Queenscliff on 22 October for a fishing holiday. A brief game concluded at Queenscliff, they went fishing near the entrance to Port Phillip Bay. On the same day the coastal vessel Rangatira, 460 tons, sailed from Melbourne. Off Queenscliff the Aboriginal anglers boarded her and, as steerage passengers, they were spirited out of the Colony. (76)

If the Aborigines had to be almost smuggled out of Australia was precisely because of the fear that their tour might not be officially sanctioned. The entire tour was too fatiguing. One player, King Cole, died of tuberculosis (by another account pneumonia) on tour. There were 47 matches played within a span of 6 months. Red Cap and Tiger playing in all of them, Cuzens in 46, Dick-a-Dick and Mulagh in 45. The players played on 99 out of 126 possible days, and travelling to matches was very time-consuming in the time period. Play began at 11:00 a.m. or noon and lasted until 7:00 p.m. or later. But it was not merely about the exhibiting of the cricket feats of the Aborigines but they were also made to showcase their talents in what was termed as "sporting exhibitions" such as 100 yard flat races, running high jump, standing high jump, 150 yard hurdles race, vaulting with poles, throwing the cricket Ball, 100 yards backwards, water bucket race, throwing the boomerangs, and spears, and kangaroo rats "by the Blacks," "Lawrence's feat with the bat and ball," and "Dick-a-Dick dodging the cricket ball". Richard Broome in an article published in the journal *Labour History* details out the same further:

> Less well-known are the other performances of the players while on tour. It was not unusual for games—running and jumping events—to be engaged in by the players and spectators after cricket matches. Mullagh and Dick-a-Dick usually won the cricket ball throwing contests with hurls of 90-100 metres. Lawrence, another member of the team, performed feats of catching a cricket ball on the blade of the bat when thrown from across the oval. Dick-a-Dick gave exhibitions of running backwards, Charley Dumas demonstrated the boomerang, and others threw the 'weet-weet', a half-a-metre stick with a knob on it used for hunting. Dick-a-Dick, armed only with a triangular shield 1 metre long by 15 centimetres wide at the centre, awed onlookers by deflecting cricket balls—often several at a time—pelted at him from 10-15 metres distance by using traditional fighting skills. At one ground he earned a shower of 50/- from the crowd for his efforts. The sports always included a mock battle. The performers, dressed

> in possum skin cap and loin cloth, threw spears at each other from 100 metres with the aid of spear-throwers—enough to impress the ethnographers, J.G. Wood and A.L. Pitt Rivers. (172)

The final scorecard for the whole team revealed that the Aboriginal team won 14 matches, lost 14 matches and there was 19 draws. Both Mullagh and Lawrence took more than 250 wickets each, and Mullagh, Cuzens and Lawrence each scored over 1,000 runs, all feats considerable even by today's standards.

Not only 8000 people flanked on the first day of the match, but also according to Mulvaney and Harcourt the players were publicly admired by English commentators as "lively and gentlemanly" and "a fine body of men"; and there were no records of the players being exploited or toured unwillingly. The last two observations brings to fore the apparent success of showcasing a set of "whitewashed" Aborigines and the Gramscian cultural "hegemony" involved in the same. Cricket, the modern sport, serves the tool of the White man's burden to civilize and modernize the primitive. Allen Guttmann, in *From Ritual to Record* (1978), identifies seven interdependent characteristics of modern sport:

> (1) secularism—participation in modern sport is rarely related to formal aspects of religious worship; (2) equality—in modern sports considerable stress is placed on the importance of equal opportunity for participation (in the sense that nobody is formally barred) and on literally and metaphorically providing participants with a 'level playing field'; (3) specialization—in modern sports we clearly distinguish between game forms and increasingly expect elite participants to specialize in terms of one particular sport, and a particular role within that sport; (4) bureaucratization—modern sports are not spontaneously organized or ad hoc, but are administered centrally, often by people who are not themselves participants; (5) rationalization—modern sports are underpinned by an instrumental rationality which leads events to be staged in specially constructed venues with increasing human control over environmental conditions, equipment which is standardized and regulated, and participants who are prepared using the latest scientific techniques and advances in knowledge; (6) quantification—in modern sport actions are translated into numerical data and participants' performances are measured, recorded and compared; and (7) the quest for records—spectators expect participants in modern sports to produce increasingly advanced

> performances through which we can see the progression of humanity. (Dominic et al. 20)

From the microcosmic level of cricket to the macrocosmic concept of Gramscian ideological *Weltanschauung* each of these qualities were meant to be absorbed by the Aborigines; and to the extent that they were absorbed through a cultural hegemony became a matter of proud parade of novelty for the White colonial pedagogues. Rightly does Marcia Langton in a radio talk observe: "The way that Aboriginal people were donned in traditional English cricket gear and lined up in teams to play opposite the white settlers was a form of racist entertainment for the white settlers. You know, they were a circus exhibit" ("Radio National—Sports Factor." *ABC*. 17/08/2001. n.pg.). On the team's first appearance at Oval, *The Times* reported:

> Their hair and beards are long and wiry, their skins vary in shades of blackness, and most of them have broadly expanded nostrils. Having been brought up in the bush to agricultural pursuits under European settlers, they are perfectly civilised and are quite familiar with the English language. ("Australian Aboriginal Cricket team in England, 1868." *Wikipedia*. n.pg.)

Rex Harcourt adds a further explanatory note:

> Well if you take the attitude of the British public, they had seen themselves, their nation, as crusaders to the Southern Hemisphere, to the savages if you like, of the Southern Hemisphere, the nether lands. They, I believe in the first instance, saw this (the Aboriginal Cricket team) as one of the first examples of the fruits of that crusade coming back to England, to the Mother Country, and demonstrating it through the medium of cricket. And there was even in one newspaper comment, which went to the extremes of saying 'Today their hand is on the cricket bat, tomorrow it might be on the plough.' In other words, learning industrious habits from the British settlers. (n.pg.)

Yet, if there is a scope for hegemony then the lack of popularity with cricket among the Aborigines reveals an undercurrent of counter hegemony. Cricket as a medium of instruction that was primarily taught through missionaries established by colonial churches dwindled away in its influence. Cricket was presented as a means to a civilized world, promoting teamwork, obedience to the rules and respect for "fair play". Cricket that was presented to customize Aborigines to white values failed to hold its sway when the team members were financially deprived and faced the stringent legislations of Aboriginal Protection Act of Victoria passed on their return in 1869. John Gemmell in "All White Mate? Cricket and Race in Oz", reminds that "of those who returned, seven spent time on a reserve, two vanished and two cannot be accounted for" (38). In his *Prison Notebooks* Gramsci talks about the dual consciousness of the masses which lays the seeds for counter-hegemony:

> Two theoretical consciousness (or one contradictory consciousness): one which is implicit in his activity and which in reality unites him with all his fellow workers in the practical transformation of the real world; and one, superficially explicit or verbal, which he has inherited from the past and uncritically absorbed. But this verbal conception is not without consequences. It holds together a specific social group, it influences moral conduct and the direction of will, with varying efficacity but often powerfully enough to produce a situation in which the contradictory state of consciousness does not permit of any action, any decision or any choice, and produces a condition of moral and political passivity. (333)

Hence one may conveniently conclude that hegemony does not always result into any sort of active commitment by the subjects to the legitimacy of the elite rule. But, where overtly breaking into protest is not possible, an oblique recourse to the same is taken. Two of the members of the Aboriginal team that returned who escaped to the bushes never to return back indicate the same. Only Johnny Mullagh remained free of reserve life. Cuzens and Mullagh were employed the following season as professionals, at the Melbourne Cricket Ground, and lived at the Melbourne Cricket Ground. Twopenny in New South Wales originally came from Bathurst and then later played cricket with Newtown, played one game for New South Wales against Victoria. It is to be remembered that "consent" for Gramsci involves a complex mental state, a "contradictory consciousness" mixing approbation and apathy, resistance and resignation. If the mix in ratio varied from individual to individual then the players such as Mullagh, Cuzens and Twopenny would be thought as more "civilized" and "socialized" than the others. Whatever the case, the ruling group was never able to engineer consent with complete success; the outlook of the subordinate group was always divided and ambiguous. Thereby, in the ultimate analysis one would concur with the views expressed by Jon Gemmell:

> Cricket filled no social role nor was it in harmony with Aboriginal values and, ultimately, many must have questioned the benefits of continuing to play. In a hostile world, the 'advantages' of the 'civilized' life did not translate into greater freedoms or economic independence. Aborigines may have learned the white man's game, but they were not rewarded with social prestige or upward mobility. Indeed, they had to seek permission from the white authorities to marry; miscegenation was outlawed and their children taken from them and made wards of the state. As Wimpress neatly summarized: 'Whites generally reneged on promises regarding cricket, as they did regarding the promised benefits of Christianity, education and work. Plainly, Aboriginal cricketers could gain no stake in the game.' (31)

No wonder Amanda Smith in the "Radio National—Sports Factor" (2001) reminds:

> And it would take another 130 years before a player of Aboriginal heritage would represent Australia at cricket again, the fast bowler Jason Gillespie who's currently playing in the Ashes series in England, and who captained the ATSIC Chairman's Eleven against the Prime Minister's Eleven, a match played in Canberra in April this year. (n.pg.)

NOTE

In a discussion between Amanda Smith and Rex Harcourt about Australian Aboriginal Cricketers tour (1867-68), Harcourt describes the straightjacketing uniform that robs the Indigenous people of their identity. Yet, the insignia on their caps could perhaps be treated as an insinuation of ambiguity in the process of white hegemonic assimilation:

Amanda Smith: Describe for us the uniform of the Aboriginal team.

Rex Harcourt: Well there's their cricket attire, which was the white flannel trousers, a red shirt, blue sash across the breast, a blue sash around their waist, and then each of the players had a distinctive cap so that they could be identified and on that cap was a brooch which showed a boomerang and a cricket bat. Now for the athletics displays the main characters were robed, you could almost describe like present-day winter underwear of long-johns and the singlet with short sleeves and so forth, for their boomerang throwing, spear throwing and so forth. (n.pg.)

WORKS CITED

Brohm, Jean-Marie. Sport: a prison of measured time, London: Pluto, 1989.

Broome, Richard. "Aboriginal Workers." *Australian Society for the Study of Labour History*. 68-69. (1995).

Dominic, Malcom et al. *The Changing Face of Cricket: From Imperial to Global Game*. Abingdon: Routledge, 2010.

Gellner, Ernest. *Nations and Nationalisms*. New York: Cornell UP, 1983.

Gemmell, Jon. "All White Mate? Cricket and Race in Oz." *Sport in Society*. 10.1: 33-48.

Gramsci, Antonio. *Selections from the Prison Notebooks*. New York: International Publishers, 1971.

Gruneau, Richard. *Class, Sports, and Social Development*. Amherst, MA: University of Massachusetts Press, 1983.

Guttmann, Allen. *From Ritual to Record: The Nature of Modern Sport*. New York: Columbia UP, 1978.

Harcourt, Rex. "Radio National—Sports Factor." *ABC*. 17/08/2001. Web. 21/08/2015.

Hargreaves, Jennifer. *Sport, Power and Culture*. New York: St Martin's Press, 1986.

Huizinga, Johan. *Homo Ludens: A Study of the Play-Element in Culture*. Boston: Beacon Press, 1955.

Hyam, Ronald. *Britain's Imperial Century, 1815-1914: A Study of Empire and Expansion*. London: Batsford, 1976.

Langton, Marcia. "Radio National—Sports Factor." *ABC*. 17/08/2001. Web. 21/08/2015.

Mulvaney, D.J. *Cricket Walkabouts: The Australian Aboriginal Cricketers on Tour 1867-68*. Melbourne: Melbourne UP, 1967.

Novak, Michael. *The Joy of Sports*. New York: Basic Books, 1976.

Schmitz, K.L. "Sport and Play: Suspension of the Ordinary." *Philosophic Enquiry in Sport*. Eds. W.J. Morgan and K.V. Meier. Champaign, Il: Human Kinetics, 1988.

Smith, Amanda. "Radio National—Sports Factor." *ABC*. 17/08/2001. Web. 21/08/2015.

Cosmic Concerns in the Plays of Obotunde Ijimere

BASAVARAJ NAIKAR

OBOTUNDE IJIMERE was the pseudonym of Horst Ulrich Beier, known as Ulli Beier (30 July 1922–3 April 2011),[1] was a German-Jewish editor, writer and scholar, who had a pioneering role in developing literature, drama and poetry in Nigeria, as well as literature, drama and poetry in Papua New Guinea. His second wife, Georgina Beier born in London, had a similarly instrumental role in stimulating the visual arts during their residencies in both Nigeria and Papua New Guinea.

While at the university, Beier transferred from the Phonetics department to the Extra-Mural Studies department. There he became interested in traditional Yoruba culture and arts. Though a teacher at Ibadan, he ventured beyond it, living in the cities of Ede, Ilobu and Osogbo, to learn more about the Yoruba communities. Due to his subsequent anthropological work among the members of the clans that are native to these places, he was awarded Yoruba honorary chieftaincies. In 1956, after visiting the First Congress of Negro Artists and Writers in Paris organized by Présence Africaine at the Sorbonne, Ulli Beier returned to Ibadan with more ideas.

In 1957 he founded the magazine *Black Orpheus*. Its name was inspired by "Orphée Noir", an essay that he had read by the French intellectual Jean Paul Sartre. The first African literary journal in English, it quickly became the leading venue for publishing contemporary Nigerian authors. It became known for its innovative works and literary excellence, and was widely acclaimed. Later in 1961, Beier co-founded the Mbari Artists and Writers Club, Ibadan, a place for new writers, dramatist and artists, to meet and perform their work. Among the young writers involved with it in the exciting early years of Nigerian independence were Chinua Achebe and Wole Soyinka. In 1962, with the dramatist Duro Ladipo, he co-founded Mbari-Mbayo, Osogbo.

Ulli Beier was also known for his work in translating traditional Nigerian literary works into English. He emerged as one of the scholars who introduced African writers to a large international audience. He translated the plays of such Nigerian dramatists as Duro Ladipo and published *Modern Poetry* (1963), an anthology of African poems.

Obotunde Ijimere, who is one of the important dramatists of Western Nigeria, has written a few plays, which are very significant from the point of view of theme and invite comparison with similar plays of other dramatists of other countries in the world. They deal not with individual or social problems but with universal issues of life as expressed in Nigerian cosmogonies. It is because of their universality that the Nigerian myths are comparable to those of other cultures like the Greek, the Christian and the Hindu and so on. It is because of the use of Nigerian myths that Obotunde Ijimere's drama appeals to the reader. His plays are comparable to the Greek tragedies, medieval Moralities and the Hindu *Puranas* as far as their simplicity, profundity and universality are concerned. As the playwright says in his *Introduction*, "Theatre in the Yoruba language is mostly a kind of opera, in which the songs are rehearsed, while the dialogue is improvised. In the late twenties and thirties this form was developed in the so-called African churches, the *Apostolic Church* and the *Seraphim and Cherubim*. The Bible stories and moralities performed by these church societies soon gave way to profane plays, social and political satires which were played by professional touring companies" (6).[2]

Myth, according to Levi-Strauss is the common language used by the primitive or savage man, who had an imaginative mind, instead of a rational or scientific mind. As Jung says, "We see the antique spirit creates not science but mythology."[3] Myth was a bricolage of understanding the world. Myth is structured on the basis of binary opposites according to Levi-Strauss.[4] Myth has to convey a moral lesson or message to mankind. That is why some scholars consider myth as "picturesque metaphysics".[5] Mircea Eliade considers myth as "sacred history" and "sacred narrative".[6]

The first play *The Imprisonment of Ọbatala* depicts the theme of contrast between war and peace in the cosmos. Based on the African myth of creation and destruction, the play celebrates the great importance of peace in the universe. As the playwright says in his "Introduction" *The Imprisonment of Obatala* is an ambitious play, which explores the philosophy of Yoruba *orisha* worship and tries to show the interplay of cosmic forces that are personified in the Yoruba imagination as *orisha*—supernatural beings, half human and historical, half divine and eternal (vi). Comparing the Brazilian and Yoruba myths Wole Soyinka points out, "In both the Yoruba and the Brazilian versions, Obatala's journey is presented as a parable of confrontation with Destiny."[7]

The characters in the play are drawn from Yoruba mythology representing different cosmic forces or energies. For example, Obatala is King of Ife and God of Creation. The setting is at once cosmic (involving Heaven and Earth) and feudal and the action is symbolic and pregnant with mythological references. The play begins with the celebration of the Festival of New Yam. This festival has been possible only because of the carriage of their sacrifice by the vulture to Heaven. Yemanja, therefore, praises the vulture for doing this holy job for them:

> Blessed be the bald patch on the head of vulture.
> Had he not carried the sacrifice to heaven,
> How could we celebrate the new yam.
> We thank the owner of the sky for this year's rain:
> We thank the earth for bowing to the sky. (Scene I. 3)

Obatala remembers his friend, Shango, King of Oyo and God of Thunder and wants to meet him after a long interval of ten years by way of courtesy and thanksgiving:

> Ten years have passed, since we have settled
> The quarrel between heaven and Earth.
> For the tenth year now, the earth has been pregnant
> With the sperm of heaven,
> Ten years, since Shango, owner of the palace,
> Met me at Ife to plead with the earth.
> How we rejoiced, when vulture rose to Heaven
> Carrying Earth's sacrifice
> And rain poured down once more
> After the long drought.
> Little we cared, that rivers of red mud
> Washed away our houses, that the wind
> Carried away the straw from our roofs
> Scattering our belongings.
> For the famine was over;
> The yam sprouted from its mounds
> Creeping up the sticks;
> Corn cobs appeared
> With the rows and rows of gleaming teeth

And cassava, with a rough skin on its back,
Swelled up in the earth, red as camwood. (Scene I. 4)

Obatala, king of Ife and god of creation wants to go to Oyo, but his wife Yemanja dissuades him from going there lest he should meet his death:

My husband:
Anybody who waits for the buffalo waits for death!
Anybody who waits for the elephant waits for death!
Do not provoke the god of fate with this rash trip.
The kingdom of Oyo is harsh. (Scene I. 5)

But since he has decided upon the trip, he consults Babalawo, the father of secrets, who alerts him about his fate and his transgression of the God of Fate, Olodumare and asks him to have patience like a rock:

Obatala,
Who turns blood into children!
Obatala, who can turn a single man into two hundred!
Divine craftsman, second only to the owner of heaven:
You have an account to settle with the God of fate.
Olodumare, the immovable rock, who never dies,
Olodumare, the eye of heaven, that does not grow any grass,
Olodumare, the owner of the sun, the sky and the earth,
Appointed you his craftsman
To mould the features of man.
Obatala who turns blood into children,
You who make nose and eyes,
You who make penis and vagina,
You betrayed the trust of Olodumare.
You drank the milky wine of the palm
Cool and sizzling it was in the morning,
Fermenting in the calabash.
Its sweet foam overflowed
Like the eyes of a woman in love.
You refreshed yourself in the morning
But by evening time your hands were unsteady,
Your senses were dull, your fingertips numbed.
And then,
You made the blind man who cannot see
The whiteness of the cattle egret,

Nor the blackness of the hornbill,
Nor the redness of the cuckal.
You made the red-eyed albino
Who is frightened of the sun,
Whose skin is sore like the leper's.
You made the hunchback,
Laughing stock of children,
Shunned by women,
A living calabash of medicine,
You must pay for your sins:
As soon as you leave this sacred city,
Eshu will be waiting for you behind the iroko tree,
He will be hidden in anthills,
You will meet him on the road and in the bush,
In the savanna and in the farm. (Scene II. 9-11)

Obatala, being alerted by Olodumare, accepts the consequences of his sin and the punishment meted out to him by his fate:

Whatever fate awaits me,
I will accept.
Whatever suffering Eshu has thought up for me
I will suffer! (Scene II. 11)

He, therefore, takes the guise of a mendicant priest and goes on his trip. Throughout the journey he acts as a man of peace and controls his temper in spite of provocation by people like Eshu. At last when he comes to the country of Oyo and tries to seize the favourite horse of Shango, he is arrested by the latter's soldiers. Shango does not recognize Obatala initially but Obatala reminds the latter about their past friendship:

It is true, ten years have passed,
Since we dispatched the vulture to heaven:
Ten years since vulture staggered
Under the weight of Earth's sacrifice.
Ten years since the two of us
Have shared the new yam that is whiter
Than the eyes of a woman in love.
And yet:
The taste of friendship lingers in the mouth
Like bitter kola nut. (Scene IV. 21)

But Shango does not care for Obatala's words of friendship even after recognizing him and insults him and accuses him of having degenerated into a thief and fool:

> Oh horror!
> Is it you, Obatala, who turns blood into children?
> Is it you, Obatala the father of laughter?
> Could I ever forget the day we danced to your sixteen drums?
> Is it possible that the wisest of all
> Should have become the most foolish?
> And the purest, the most foul?
> Oh horror, the father of laughter,
> Who rides the hunchback, has turned
> A common thief. (Scene IV. 21)

Shango is not aware of the disaster that he has invited upon his land by imprisoning Obatala. Oya, wife of Shango warns him against the ill treatment of Obatala. But Shango turns a deaf ear to her words and orders, "Take him to prison and out of my sight!" (Scene IV. 23). Now Obatala senses the operation of the god of fate and relents and is ready to face the consequences of his acts:

> Shango—
> How I had longed for this day!
> But Eshu the weaver of fate
> Has confused the threads.
> Now I must wait
> For him to disentangle them himself.
> Eshu who turns right into wrong;
> Wrong into right. (Scene IV. 24)

Shango is not ready to accept the Obatala's transgressive act of stealing his favourite horse; He therefore justifies his punishment of the criminal before his wife, Oya:

> It must have been the wisdom of his elders
> That prevented Obatala from being a fool.
> What madness to steal a horse he cannot ride
> Like an impotent old chief
> Who marries a moist young wife
> And hides the shriveled fruit
> Between his legs.
> Oh, had he tried to mount

This quivering black flame
He would have shook him off
Even quicker than the frustrated wife
Got rid of her limp husband
Who lacked the tool
To make her bleed and sweat. (Scene IV. 24)

But Oya reminds her husband that he has done an unjust act by imprisoning Obatala and that it would bring dire consequences to their kingdom:

My Lord,
Even now the imprisonment of Obatala spells disaster.
The bringer of peace, the father of laughter is in jail,
You have unleashed Ogun, who bathes in blood.
Even now his rain begins:
He kills suddenly in the house and suddenly in the field.
He kills the child with the iron with which it plays.
Ogun kills the owner of the slaves and the slaves as well.
He kills the owner of the house and paints the hearth with his blood!
(Scene IV. 27)

Since Ogun, the war god is at the height of his excitement, the war breaks out suddenly in Oyo and consequently Shango has to take his sword to fight in the battle with Obatala. Meanwhile the land of Oyo is slowly affected by an unknown curse as a result of which no pregnant woman is able to be delivered of a child or survive the childbirth. The whole land is thus reduced to a sterile one. Shocked by this unexpected danger, Shango grows restless and consults Babalawo who attributes the operation of the curse to the imprisonment of Obatala, the apostle of peace:

Father of secrets
Throw your palm nuts,
Draw your secret symbols into flour
And chant your sacred verse
To let us know:
Why our children die and why crops fail!
Teach us the sacrifice and spells,
Concoctions, prayers and actions
That may break the curse. (Scene IV. 33)

At last Shango realizes his folly, apologizes to Obatala:

> Oh father of laughter!
> I was like the patient who was cured
> And beat his doctor.
> I was foolish like the knife
> That destroys its own sheath.
> Father:
> Many words do not fill a basket.
> The most beautiful speech
> Falls like water through wickerwork
> Oh father of laughter
> Try to forgive the injustice done to you. (Scene V. 35-36)

Shango thus releases Obatala, who forgives him instantly because of his magnanimity by explaining his own fault. Thus both of them repent of their crimes or sins for which they have suffered in their own ways. Obatala describes the element of fate in very beautiful manner:

> He who admits his fault
> Will not be kept kneeling for long.
> When death is not ready to receive somebody
> He will send him a doctor at the right time.
> So here I am at last
> Beholding the fire in your eyes again.
> Shango
> My suffering was not your doing.
> I had an account to settle
> With the God of fate.
> The owner of heaven has not forgiven me
> For in my drunkenness
> I had made the Albino
> Whose bleached skin is sore like the lepers,
> I had made the hunchback
> To whom women close their thighs
> And the blind man
> Who is helpless like a bat in sunlight.
> Eshu, confuser of men,
> Has brought my suffering about.
> Throwing a stone today
> He killed a bird yesterday;

But let us now rejoice:
The taste of friendship lingers in the mouth
Like bitter kola nut.
Friendship like lost virginity
Can never be undone.
True friendship never takes offence:
I asked you to be patient,
You were wildly impatient
And I loved you for it.
I asked you to be peaceful,
You steeped your arms in blood
But I still loved you for it. (Scene V. 35-36)

Now peace is restored as the conflict between Shango and Obatala results into reconciliation, repentance, forgiveness and peace. Eshu, the God of fate rests content after having done his cosmic duty. Ogun, the god of war begins to take rest with a sense of contentment. The play based upon the African myth, with a cosmic worldview, obviously depicts the necessity, importance and creativity of peace and the undesirability and destructiveness of war—lesson universally relevant to the world, especially in the modern days of international power politics, cold war and atomic war. It easily brings to our mind the atmosphere of the Greek tragedies. This principle is as true in the cosmic world as in the natural and the human world. The myth of the play, in spite of being primitive in nature is quite contemporary in its appeal and relevance. The modern world, which has seen two wars, can easily understand the meaning of the play.

The second play *Everyman* also is cosmic in its setting though the central theme highlights the human obsession with money. The African gods and their dealings in Heaven are presented in their relation to human life. Olodumare (Who is almost equal to Lord Siva) the god in Heaven is angry with Everyman (who is almost equal to *jivatma* of the Hindu philosophy) for forgetting Him and pursuing money and woman:

Truly I am tired of the children of the world.
Their origin in haven they forget—
Living worse than beasts.
I gave them eyes—they refuse to see.
I gave them ears—they refuse to hear.
I gave them brains—they refuse to remember.

Look at Everyman enjoying his wealth.
He has children, he has houses, he has lorries:
And his money increases and his children;
And his money multiplies and has grandchildren.
But he forgets,
Money does not prevent a man from becoming a fool.
Money does not prevent a man from becoming mad.
The red feather is the pride of the parrot.
The young leaf is the pride of the palm tree.
The sun is the pride of heaven:
But wisdom—not money—is the pride of man! ("Prologue in Heaven," 47-48)

Everyman is conscious of his wealth and its dynamism to get everything done, possessed and enjoyed by its owner. His philosophy of money is exactly like that of Karl Marx. He is very proud of his money:

In all the town there is none
More respected than I.
My money multiplies daily,
There is nobody in this town
Whom I could not buy! When
I enter the palace, the drummers
Forget the praise names of the king
And let the air resound with my name:
Everyman, commander of money,
Everyman, owner of the town,
Everyman, owner of the world! (50)

Everyman spends most of his time in the company of a Harlot, a Fat Cousin and so on. He arranges a grand party for his guests including his lady-love, the Harlot. He sends a wad of dollar notes to Bisi so that she may decorate herself grandly and attend his party. He instructs his companion to the following bidding:

You my friend and companion of many years,
Take this money, and hurry down to Bisi,
My lady-lover. Tell her to come to my party
And bring the best Highlife band
She can find. And give her these few notes—
For these independent women and
Lip-painted ladies have many needs

And great pride. Let her go and buy
What she desires and let heart
Be happy when she comes. (51)

Everyman who is willing to spend such a big amount on the party for his guests, is not willing to help a poor neighbour who is badly in need of money. He throws just a piece of three penny coin to the neighbour, who refuses to take it. Then Everyman expresses the difficulties of rich men in general. His views are as callous as interesting. He tells the poor man as follows:

You foolish man!
Do you know what it means to be a rich man?
Do you think it is easy?
'A rich man!' That is easily said.
But we rich people lead a hard life,
If you know it,
You might not want to change with me.
My money can never sit still:
It must run here and there,
Work for me and travel and fight.
Money must marry more money
And get pregnant with more money.
A rich man has no easy life:
His lorries break down
And want to be mended.
The price of cocoa falls
And petrol goes up.
One's children go to school
They study abroad, their dowry
Must be paid when they marry.
Do you think it is easy to maintain
All these houses and cars and farms
The children and wives and servants?
Do you think that money grows on a tree?
No work is harder than collecting debts and rents!
If I would listen to fellows like you,
I could not make three steps
Without opening my hand.
You think it is easy! But suppose

All my property was divided equally
Among all those who are in need—
Do you think your share would be bigger,
Than these three pence here? (53)

He throws away the coins of three-pence at his poor neighbour, who helplessly picks them up and goes away. Then a policeman brings in a debtor, who has not been able to repay the loan that he has borrowed from Everyman. The debtor apologizes for the delay of repayment due to his poverty and requests for some more time for clearing the loan. But Everyman acts very callously by refusing to allow any more time to the debtor. When the debtor curses him he gives him a long lecture on the sanctity and importance of the economics of money and its transaction, which is very interesting:

You are quick to curse like a fool!
Why do you pretend to despise money?
Money was your *orisha*, money was your oracle,
Money was your father, money was your mother.
Why do you try to renounce it now?
Blessed is the day when money was invented!
Money has power over any other thing:
There is no house, no land, no wife it cannot buy.
Money is more powerful than judges and kings.
Money is the most faithful servant
To the man who owns it. (55)

He callously asks the policeman to carry the debtor off to prison. The wife and children of the debtor follow them weeping. Thus Everyman drunk with the power of money has grown indifferent and insensitive to other people's troubles and problems.

Having dismissed the debtor Everyman gets ready to expect his guests for the party and the forthcoming enjoyment and excitement. But the very sound of music ironically saddens his heart the exact reason of which he cannot understand at all. He begins to worry about his sudden feeling of depression:

Everyman the money commander,
Everyman owner of the town, owner of the world!
But something oppresses me today.
The very thought of music makes me sad.
The thought of drink even makes me sick.

Yet I am not ill—
Something spoils my pleasure today:
Something worries my head—
Something like fear.
But why should I feel fear?
No man was more secure than I.
Nobody dares to raise his hand against me:
I buy and sell them all.
No beautiful women will refuse my love—
I buy and sell them all. Yet I am sad today? (56)

In spite of his self-analysis, Everyman feels a sense of fear and is tempted to consult an oracle priest, Babalawo, who is passing by that route. He talks insultingly and contemptuously to the priest, but yet wants to know the reason for his sudden depression. He gives him a small coin and asks him to throw his nuts and utter his prophesy:

Throw your nuts…
Let me hear your lies,
It will pass the time,
While I wait for my guests. (57)

Accordingly the Babalawo kneels down and spreads out his utensils on the floor. He throws his palm-nuts and draws his signs in the sand. Then he recites his Odu, and tells him indirectly through a moral tale of the importance of sacrifice and the punishment for not carrying out the sacrifice. But Everyman animadverts him as an impudent old rascal, father of lies trying to frighten him with the fear of death.

Turning a deaf ear to the Babalawo's prediction, Everyman proceeds to immerse himself in the enjoyment of the party with his guests. There is band music played to accompany their party. He admires the Harlot's beauty poetically:

You are the blackest girl in town,
Your neck is longer, your hips are rounder
Than any other girl's
You make me forget my fifty years,
You make me feel young and gay like a boy. (58)

But when is all the guests are enjoying the party. He suddenly begins to behave crazily and embarrassingly. For example he thanks them:

Thank you, thank you my friends all,
For coming to lead me to my grave. (59)

His subconscious fear of death seems to come to the surface and he talks what he should not intend to. The Harlot tries to convince the people that Everyman is feeling rather feverish and that people should not misunderstand him. When the band music is sounded he begins to have unmentionable fear. He thinks that the god of death is calling him:

My God, who is calling me
With this terrible voice?
My friends, my friends,
Who is calling so? (63)

His premonition has come true. He hears the supernatural voice, which is not heard by other participants in the party. At last Iku, the God of Death appears and questions him:

Everyman! Can you enjoy yourself,
With music and drink and harlots,
And forget your creator? (64)

He asks Everyman to give an account of his life before the throne of Olodumare, but the latter confesses that his book of accounts is not yet ready and that he should be granted a little more time. But Iku does not grant his request. However after a lot of persuasion, Iku grants him an hour's time to get ready to die. Within that short time of an hour Everyman asks his friends like Companion, Fat Cousin, Thin Cousin to accompany him to heaven along with him and help him give an account of his life to Lord Olodumare, but they refuse to oblige him on some pretext or the other.

At last Everyman orders his servant to bring the box of money and keep it ready to be carried to heaven along with him. He requests Owo, the god of money not to desert him and with his help he can face any judgement and undertake any journey. But Owo jumps from the box of money in the personified form and taunts him:

Did I not fool you all your life?
How big, you felt yourself—
Owner of properties, owner of men.
You bought and sold, you commanded and ruled.
Like a peacock you strutted around,
Who displays his feathers to his hens.

Now you are naked and alone
Like the newly born swallow fallen from its nest,
Where are your friends, your harlots now?
Was I your slave?
Well now: you'll make your trip,
Alone, a small and naked fool.
I'll stay right here—to play with other men.
(*He pushes Everyman down—and leaves*) (71-72)

Finally his old friend, Good Deeds comes and declares that he is an embodiment of Everyman's good deeds and wants to follow him to Heaven, but now he is too old to do that, and that he was unnecessarily neglected by Everyman:

I'm your good works, I cam to follow you
On your long trip.
Before the throne of Heaven
I cam to witness on your behalf.
Alas, I am too weak.
Throughout your life, you have neglected me,
Now I am old and sick
And I can go no farther. (72)

Now Everyman realizes his folly and repents of his irrational indulgence in sensuous pleasures of life without discharging his moral duties assigned to him by God. This self-examination followed by self-realization is quite in keeping with the didactic intention of the play:

Oh what a fool I was—you my true friend
I have neglected all my life.
I loved Owo too much, the false friend
Who has now deserted me. He fooled my senses
Made me blind with drink, proud with possessions
Vain with women, drunk with power.
Oh he made me waste my life.
Empty handed and friendless now,
Must I confront Olorum now?
Woe unto me:
My promises were broken—my life was wasted
And to the potsherd heaven shall I be condemned. (72)

Then his daughter, Sidikatu meets him and confesses her feelings towards him. She thanks him for giving her a secure life but complains that he never had enough time to spend with her or care for her and that he, who was almost a second god to her, has now shrunk to such a miserable condition. She complains further that he has betrayed the trust of the God in Heaven and broken his promises. Everyman, who had insulted everyone in his life due to his intoxication with money, has now been reduced to the same position in which he is insulted or deserted by his so-called near ones and dear ones. Everyman is completely humiliated into an awareness of his unworthiness now. He wants to pray to the God in Heaven to grant me another life and to bless the child in his daughter's womb so that through he may have another beginning or birth in which to repair his present degeneration. He learns his lesson like a tragic hero but it is too late now. At this moment Iku comes and strikes him. Everyman screams and falls dead and Sadikatu breaks into wailing.

Sidikatu, who has learnt a lesson from her father's example, does not want to repeat his highhanded materialist behaviour. Now being delivered of a baby boy, she, therefore, consults Babalawo, the father of secrets and requests him to throw his nuts and predict her son's future and seeks his advice in making his life a joyous one, unlike that of his grandfather, i.e. Everyman:

> Father of secrets:
> Your nuts portend poverty and suffering
> For my child. But I will do as you say:
> I will sacrifice and pray, that the child
> Though poor, shall be good; that the child
> Though penniless shall be loved. (76)

Then as suggested by the father of secrets, she names her baby boy as Babatunde and wants to have a new beginning of life for her son. She wants her son to choose wisdom and lead a happy life rather than choose money and ruin his life: She is obviously full of this moral and spiritual awareness now:

> Orunmila, owner of heaven, be praised!
> Praised by the owner of the sun
> For granting us a new beginning!
> Olodumare,
> Nobody knows your father,
> The liars are only lying!
> Nobody knows your mother,
> The liars are only lying.

You gave us a new beginning!
You will see another life:
For Owo shall be banished from this child's life:
Greed, avarice and lust for power
Shall be driven from his doorstep!
For he has come back to think again
And to choose anew:
If poverty sits on his head—he will not care.
If hunger hangs round his neck—he will not mind.
If nakedness uncovers his bottom—he will not be ashamed.
For he has come to choose wisdom—the pride of man. (76-77)

Sadikatu's choice of wisdom rather than material wealth for her son is approved by the Chorus, which is equivalent to the voice of God and society in general:

Babatunde O!
A new beginning has been granted.
Let the child remember
That the red feathers are the pride of the parrot;
The horns are the pride of the bull;
The stars are the pride of the sun;
The spots are the pride of the leopard;
That loyalty is the pride of the dog—
But wisdom is the pride of man. (77-78)

The play, obviously, satirizes the human obsession with money and exposes it in the fashion of a fable. The play, though articulated in the form of an African myth, is universal in its relevance to the modern world, which is steeped in materialism. Money, which is the most common obsession with mankind all through the human history, has been portrayed here as inadequate for the attainment of ultimate happiness.

The third play *Woyangi* again is based on an Ijaw myth recorded by Gabriel Okara. It has the cosmic background again and the characters are drawn from both the human world and the divine world. Hence there is a lot of supernatural element in it. As myth is said to be a universal language, it is rooted in a particular culture and religion (here in this case, African) but yet applicable and appreciable universally all over the world. It easily corresponds to the Greek drama and the English Morality Play. The play depicts the theme of the contrast between fertility and barrenness as expressed in the Ijaw myth.

The play begins with the creative powers of the goddess Woyengi. Her stature is cosmic. Her powers are enumerated by the Swordbearers as follows:

Woyengi
Mother of the world,
You are bright and radiant like the sun
When it rises in the east.
Your feet walk the earth
While your head towers the sky.
You command the sun and the moon
You created the earth
When you were lonely.
You made thousands of creatures
From your single form.
You create the child
In the mother's womb,
You make the seed flow in man
And the blood in woman.
You nurse the child in the womb
You give it breath
You open its mouth
On the day of its birth
And let it speak.
You created the Niger
That flows to the sea in multiple streams
You placed the other Niger in the sky
That it may fall down and water the land.
Woyengi,
Mother of the world,
Your feet walk the earth
While your head towers in the sky. (81-82)

The goddess of creation allows the creatures to be born on the earth and also to choose their wish or fate and behave accordingly in the mortal world:

My creatures, approach
The world is waiting for you
With forests, rivers, towns and villages.
The heat of the sun you will feel

And the coolness of rain.
The land is there for you to work,
The forest to hunt in.
You will know the pain of birth,
The terror of death and the happiness of love.
Come now and choose your fate.
But choose wisely:
Nobody can eat the words
He will speak here and now.
Once you have entered the world,
Creaming, through your mother's womb,
Your words will have lost the power of creation.
But for this brief moment between creation and birth
You share with me the power of the word.
Every wish you utter
Before you wade into the world
Through the river of life
Must come to pass.
Approach, then, my creatures,
And choose your fate.
Choose—but choose wisely:
Whether man or woman you wish to be,
What manner of life you wish to lead,
What to achieve on earth, how long to live—
And finally—most difficult choice of all—You must select your death. (82-83)

As per Goddess Woyengi's order the first creature requests her to make him a warrior, i.e. a real man. He chooses to be a brave warrior and conquer the world by his sword and also die by the sword. The goddess grants his wish. The second creature requests the goddess to grant him the life of a man rooted in the soil, i.e., an agriculturist so that he could live a long life and see his children work the land and have his grandchildren to bury him when he dies quietly in his sleep. The third creature requests the goddess to grant her wish to be a fertile mother:

Woyengi,
Mother of the world—
Let me be a mother.
Let me be fruitful, and bear children

One, two, six, eight—
Let me bear children until my womb dries up. (85)

The goddess grants her wish without any hesitation. The fourth creature asks for an unusual grant. She asks the goddess to make her a barren woman:

Let me be a woman—but let my womb be dry.
Little I care for the children or wealth.
Let me learn the secrets of herbs and leaves;
Teach me the language of the cockerel and the hornbill.
Let me have power to heal and to kill.
Give me command over the word,
Let me mould the lives of men in my hand. (86)

The goddess is really surprised by this creatures' wish and yet she grants the latter's wish after articulating her sense of surprise:

Bold is your wish:
Unheard of your desire.
Yet so be it.
Arise and take your life.
But when you wade into the world
You shall not follow your fellow creatures
Through the muddy river of happiness and wealth.
You alone shall walk through the clear waters
Of the spirit. Your road shall be lonely and cold—
But your wish shall be fulfilled. (86-87)

Obboinba makes the right use of her healing powers and cures an old woman and an old man of their illnesses. But when she goes to Lapke's house and observes the latter's children playing the games happily and noisily she feels jealous of Lapke's joys of motherhood. She stops eating her food offered by Lapke in the middle as she cannot bear the pangs of jealousy. She jumps up and bursts out:

I cannot bear it,
I cannot bear it any longer!
To see you swell up with child nearly every two years
To see you surrounded by eight children
And for me to have none. Not even a single one!
I cannot bear to see the happiness in your eyes
To stand by and watch with my shriveled womb!

I hate myself, my cursed body,
Unable to have even an abortion.
I will not suffer it
I will not bear my shame another day!
I shall return to Woyengi and challenge my fate! (93)

Lapke understand her feelings and reminds her that she has chosen her fate, which cannot be reversed now. She even volunteers to offer her one of her own children for good. But Ogboinba feels the pangs of jealousy and also repent of having made the wrong choice in her life. Although she has the power to cure as well as kill people, and has power, fame and respect, she does not enjoy them as she suffers from unbearable loneliness. She, therefore, decides to go back to Woyengi:

So let me go to Woyengi!
I'll challenge her
And she must recreate my fate! (93)

Before going to Goddess Woyengi, Ogboinba meets Isembi, the king of the forest and challenges him to prove his strength. Although Isembi initially seems to triumph over her, finally he seems to grow weaker in the face of her magical powers. Ogboinba feels triumphant but spares his life thereby leaving him helpless:

Fool
I will spare your life, though you don't deserve it!
Stay in your forest: a king without power;
An impotent ruler, writhing like the broken tail
Of a lizard! (97)

(*Ogboinba moves out triumphantly—followed by all the powers*)

Then Ogboinba goes to Olokun, the king of the sea and challenges him to prove his strength. Although she is initially defeated by him, finally she emerges triumphant due to her magical powers. She, therefore, taunt him as follows:

Flap your fins then, like the helpless flounder
Thrown on the beach!
No one can stand between me and Woyengi!
Helpless king of the waters—
Frightened now, of your own sharks! (100)

Similarly Ogboinba goes to the kingdom of the Cock and vanquishes him with the help of her magical powers. Her continuous success in her encounters with these three persons has seems to have gone to her head. She therefore goes straight to Goddess Woyengi and boasts of her victories and even commands her to reshape her fate, her life and her womb. Goddess Woyengi is so angry with her arrogance that she declares that the latter, who has challenged the heaven itself, is not fit to live and wants to punish her by hurling her sword at her. But somehow Ogboinba escapes from the stroke of the sword, flees for her life and hides herself in the pregnant woman's (Lapke's) eyes. Goddess Woyengi declares her final curse on her as follows:

> So there you are hiding!
> In a pregnant woman's eyes!
> Clever you are to the last,
> Knowing I will not break my own law
> And hurt a pregnant woman!
> Well then, so be it!
> Live in the woman's eyes.
> But know that never more
> Will you lead a life of your own,
> Never be given another beginning.
> May you lead an existence of fear
> Peeping out of other people's eyes,
> They will see you staring at them
> And remember your mad adventure.
> Never more man shall be so bold! (108)

Now that the arrogant creatures like Ogboinba are vanquished by the goddess and her swollen pride is justly punished. The play obviously, depicts the triumph of fertility and creativity over barrenness and destructiveness in Nature. Now everybody accepts the omnipotence, creativity and cosmic supremacy of Goddess Woyengi. This acceptance and affirmation of her powers is articulated by the Chorus at the end of the play.

All these plays deal with the issues that encompass the whole universe and not necessarily confined to any race or nation. The generality of the appeal of these plays is achieved by the dramatists through the employment of African myths, which act as means of objectivization of the authorial vision. The technique of allegorization helps the authors to liberate the myths from the African background and extend them to the entire mankind in general. That is the reason why these plays achieve the features of the Greek Drama. Ijimere accomplishes this universality mainly through allegorisation and typicalization of characters and situations. In *The Imprisonment of Obatala* the characters like Obatala is the god of creation who corresponds to the Greek Zeus, the Biblical Yahweh and the Hindu Brahma. Shango, the god of thunder roughly corresponds to Lord Indra of the Hindu pantheon. Eshu, the god of fate corresponds to Lord Viswakarma, celestial carpenter and Ogun, god of war reminds us of the Greek Mars and the Hindu planetary deity, Mangala. Likewise the characters of *Everyman* parallel the gods of other cultures. Olodumare corresponds to the Greek Zeus, the Christian God and the Hindu Brahma. Iku easily reminds us of Lord Yama and Owo, though a god is a male equivalent of the Hindu goddess Laxmi. "Good Deeds" instantly brings to our mind the Hindu philosophical concept of "satkarmas". Likewise Everyman is a reminder of the same character in the medieval *Moralities*. The characters of *Woyengi* also have easy parallels in other cultures. Woyengi who is a goddess of creation corresponds to the Hindu goddess Sakti, incarnation of the dynamic principle in the universe. Isembi and Olokun correspond to the Hindu personifications like Vanadevata and Jaladevata. The African characters such as these represent the abstract qualities or principles like fertility, creation, barrenness, death, money-mindedness, etc. Sometimes they stand for the entire class, type or species of their kind like, for example, man, sea, forest, harlot and cousin etc. It is because of the typicality of characters and the universality of situations that they assume allegorical stature. The ideas or images of Man and God; creation and destruction; heaven and hell; forest and sea; and war, etc. presented in these plays belong to the archetypes of world literature. It is an account of these allegorical, cosmic and archetypal characters and events that Ijimere's plays invite comparison with the Greek Drama, the medieval English Moralities and the Hindu Puranas. These plays are an evidence of Ijimere's ability to depict universal patterns of thought and feeling through the African myths.

REFERENCES

1. Ulli Beier-the free encyclopedia.htm.9/4/2013.
2. Ijimere, Obotunde, *The Imprisonment of Obatala and Other Plays*, London: Arnold Heinemann, 1978. (All the page references are to this edition.)
3. Jung, C.G. *Psychology of the Unconscious*, London: Kegan Paul, Trench, Trubner & Co. Ltd. Fifth Impression, 1946, 42.

4. Quoted by Derrida, Jacques, “Structure, Sign and Play”, *Contemporary Criticism: An Anthology*, Ed. V.S. Sethuraman. Chennai: Macmillan Company of India, Reprint, 1998, 304.
5. Quoted by Chase, Richard, “Notes on the Study of Myth,” *Twentieth Century Criticism*, Eds. William J. Handy & Max Westbrook, New Delhi: Light and Life Publishers, 245.
6. Quoted by Handoo, Lalita, *Folk and Myth*, Mysore: Central Institute of Indian Languages, 1998, 33.
7. Soyinka, Wole, *Myth, Literature and the African World,* Cambridge: Cambridge University Press, Reprint 1999, 20.

The Audible Silence: Voices From The Dark

SAMIRA SINHA

NGUGI WA THIONG'O writes "Literature does not grow or develop in a vacuum; it is given impetus, shape, direction and even area of concern by social, political and economic forces in a particular society. The relationship between creative literature and these other forces cannot be ignored, especially in Africa, where modern literature has grown against the gory background of European imperialism and its changing manifestations: slavery, colonialism and neo-colonialism."[1] The colonial mindset that marginalizes the indigene as the 'other' can be internal or external, but it has the same decimating effect. It dispossesses, oppresses, and marginalizes, reducing the oppressed to a subdued, silent minority. For instance the Aborigine in Australia, the Blacks in Africa, African Americans, Amerindians, Maoris in New Zealand and the Natives of Canada, have all had to contest the construed notion of the inferior and the uncivilized. They have exposed the racist prejudice inherent in colonial discourse through their writings. The pen has given power to their anger and protest, breaking their silence and consolidating a body of literature whose ideologies and aesthetics were different from European or mainstream aesthetics.

Aboriginal poetry in the 1960s opened a new, hitherto, undefined area in Australian literature; while African writers, after the Second World War, made a conscious attempt to step up their cultural activities to assist in the struggle for freedom. This paper seeks to juxtapose some major points of reference in both Aboriginal and African literature. A brief account, however, of the colonization in Australia and Africa is essential, to appreciate their meeting points which reflect the pain of the sons of the soil, who were unjustly displaced in their native lands.

On an ill-fated day, in the late eighteenth century, Captain Cook discovered Australia, and recorded in his diaries, that unlike other tribes, the native Aborigines led a simple and peaceful life. During those days America had refused to accept shipments of British prisoners, and the British parliament in search of a place to deport and dump their convicts, seized this opportunity to turn Australia into a penal colony. They ruled

'Terra Nullius', that is, land belonging to no one, for almost two hundred years, brushing aside the legal and sentimental claims of the Aborigines. The Eurocentric bias of most Australian historians ensured the 'black out' of the Aborigines, relegating them to a place of little more than a melancholy footnote in the nation's history, conveniently ignored or glossed over, and made almost invisible. It was only after the 1960s when historians like Henry Reynolds ('Aborigines and Settlers' and 'The Other Side of the Frontier'), W.E.H. Stanner ('After the Dreaming') as well as writers like Wayne Atkinson and Kevin Gilbert spotlighted Aboriginal history, the value of understanding Australian history from the Aboriginal perspective was recognized.

European powers entered Africa, with an excuse of 'civilizing' the savages, the 'dark continent' which they associated with the illiteracy, mysterious primitivism, dark skin and black magic of the natives. Research, however, has revealed that like many an ancient civilization, for instance India, Egypt and China, Africa had also its own culture and civilization. Struck by the vast tracts of fertile land, the explorers settled in what came to be known as 'white highlands'. The Africans were then declared as 'squatters' in their own land and permitted to cultivate only small plots called 'shamba' under severe and oppressive restrictions, leading to economic and political exploitation. Several African tribes acted and reacted to the violence of European Imperialists, who drove the reluctant but subdued native by whips and gunpowder on the cotton fields of America, rubber plantations in the Congo and the gold mines in Southern Africa.

The people of these two continents, though separated by the vast Indian Ocean, shared a common destiny. The writers rose in response to the socio-political realities and human suffering and gave voice to the 'silent', 'subdued' minority and strength to the weak as a mark of solidarity. The borders of Africa and Australia seemed to dissolve, as their poets collectively spoke in one human voice of protest to reclaim their land and identity. While Aboriginal literature expressed emotional anguish, tumult of the mind and conflict between the old and the new, it was seen as an important means for the maintenance and extension of Aboriginal confidence, establishing cultural nationalism and Aboriginal pride. Similarly, African literature was also an outcry against oppression and brutalized sensibility caused by racism and was seen as a means of harnessing African aspirations in a bid to build a new country and sing a new song.

Pope John Paul II in an address at Alice Springs, to the Aboriginal and Torres Strait Islander people, on November 20, 1986, emphasized the distinctive resilience and solidarity of the Black Australian with these words:

> You have kept your sense of brotherhood..., you are like a tree standing in the middle of a bush-fire sweeping through the timber. The leaves are scorched and the tough bark is scarred and burned; but inside the tree the sap is still flowing, and under the ground the roots are still strong. Like that tree you have endured the flames, and you still have the power to be reborn.[2] (Canberra, 1986. 4)

Prophetic as these words are, rebirth had already begun in the 1960s. Oodgeroo Noonuccal's first collection of poetry, 'We Are Going', appeared in print in 1964, breaking the centuries old Aboriginal silence. This initiated a new phase of cultural communication and the birth of Fourth World Literature in Australia. Several socio-political changes altered the status of the Aboriginal Australian which led to the finding of not only their voice but also their votes, on being granted franchise. Various movements and strikes demanding equal wages and tribal land rights and the concept of the Australian Nation rattled white Australians, such as Geoff McDonald, whose book, *Red Over Black: Behind the Aboriginal Land Rights* is full of racist absurdity and inaccurate facts; or, for that matter, Hugh Morgan, an executive of the Western Mining Corporation, who in 1984 maligned the concept of land claims and protection of the sacred sites.

In their struggle for the revival of confidence and self worth; cultural nationalism and Aboriginal pride, writers like Oodgeroo Noonuccal, Kevin Gilbert and Jack Davis became role models and the spokes persons of their race. Thus Aboriginal literature became the loci for Aboriginal pride. The fact that Black Australian literature was based on the experience of the writers only added much to its power and impact; experiences which were similar to other hunter-gatherer cultures in continents as diverse as America (Indians), Africa (e.g. Tribesmen of the Kalahari) and Asia (tribal of India; Ainu of Japan). The question of identity, the anguish of discrimination and abuse as well as the struggle for land and forest rights are the dominant concerns of these people and the literature of the Fourth World.

The anti-colonial wars which began in Madagascar in 1947 and later continued in Southern Africa; the civil wars in Angola and Nigeria;

the rise of many brutal dictatorships—some still flourishing (the most recent freedom being that of Libya) and the imprisonment of Africa's most passionate and eloquent writers gave rise to a literature in which the note of loss predominates. Loss of liberty, of life, of the hopes and companions of one's youth, runs through African literature like a flood. Yet, just as in Aboriginal literature, it is strongly challenged by other assertions of what is immemorial in the African experience and has survived all the ravages of oppression and discrimination—an equal insistence upon continuity and tradition, a sense of youth, of new beginnings and untried possibilities. The writers obviously feel that their task is not just to lament their tragic and often irrevocable losses, but to identify the points of growth and renewal in the world, which is well expressed in these opening lines of the Angolan poet Augustinho Neto, in his poem 'Farewell at the Moment of Parting':

> My mother
> (Oh black mothers whose children have departed)
> You taught me to wait and to hope
> As you have done through the disastrous hours.[3]
> (*The Penguin Book of Modern African Poetry*, 27)

In another poem, 'The Grieved Lands', Neto further writes:

> The grieved lands of Africa
> In the tearful woes of ancient and modern slave....
> In the infamous sensation of the stunning perfume of the Flower
> Crushed in the forest
> By the wickedness of iron and fire.[4] (*Ibid.*, 29)

This compares well with the poem of Oodgeroo Noonuccal, 'We are Going', where similar sentiments resonate. She strongly condemns the rubbish over half-covered traces of the 'old bora ring', and laments the desecration of the sacred 'old bora ground', 'where now many white men hurry about like ants'. The bora ring and ground are used for worshipping, community gatherings and coming of age ceremonies. 'A semi-naked band subdued and silent' stands as mute spectators of the destruction of their homeland and traditional customs by the white intruders. Both the poems end on a strong note of assertion and sense of identity. Noonuccal further avers:

> We belong here, we are of the old ways.
> We are the corroboree and the bora ground.[5]
> (*Modern Australian Poetry*, 69)

Neto on the other hand asserts:

They live
the grieved lands of Africa
in the harmonious sound of consciences
contained in the honest blood of men……
because we are living
and are imperishable particles
of the grieved lands of Africa.[6] (*Penguin*, 30)

Rex Ingamells in his poem 'History', harks back at the arrival of the white intruders when "Pioneer ships lumbering in the sunset", loaded with men "fierce in their misery" brought destruction to his homeland, Australia. He perceives how "Herds of cattle, lowing by the fertile banks/ of eastern rivers" are converted into:

Deserted station houses, quiet in drought.
Bones of cattle, camels, horses, men,
And the despised black who lives through it all.[7]
(*Australian Literature*, 70)

Jean-Baptiste Tati-Loutard of the Congo Republic, in a similar vein decries

The insult and darkness of refusal—
I remember it through the navel
Which ties me to the centuries of wrong.[8] (*Penguin*, 70)

Adam Shoemaker in his book, *Black Words White Page*, observes that both multinational mining and Black Australian poetry are activities which are very important to the Aboriginal Australian writer, whose sense of pride and confidence is engendered by writing, expressing and publishing his innermost feelings and anguish while coming into contact with European technology, mining and politics. Black Australian poetry and African poetry both, undoubtedly, point towards indiscriminate exploitation of their land reserves and people by the white settlers. Gray Bostock's poem, entitled 'An Australian Miner', sardonically reveals:

A young Australian Miner
Sat in his company's diner
Having coffee and yellow cake;
He seemed quite amused
By the Black's land he'd abused
In the National Interest's sake.[9] (Shoemaker, 265)

Noemia de Sousa, an African poet, who writes of a fellow countryman, Magaica's losses in the mines of Rand laments:

And, stunned
Magaica lit a lamp
to search for his lost illusions
for his youth and health which stay buried
deep in the mines of Johannesburg.
Youth and health,
the lost illusions
which shine like stars
on some lady's neck in some City's night.[10] (*Penguin*, 19)

These two perspectives, though emanating from either side of the dark continents, voice the same sentiment, the same outrage. Like olives, writers yield their best in times of oppression. In looking beyond the 'self', he widens the horizon of his vision and encounters, in the process, new realities, raising his work from the 'local' to the 'global', that is, the universal.

The findings of the Muirhead Royal Commission lent political strength to aboriginal deaths in custody. Robert Walker, a black victim of custodial death, describes the brutalities imposed on him inside the prison in his poem titled 'Inside Black Australia':

Have you ever heard screams in the middle of the night,
Or the sobbing of a stir-crazy prisoner,
Echo over and over again in the darkness—
Threatening to draw you into its madness?[11] (Shoemaker, 270)

Walker's indignation and sense of horror at 'This rehabilitation system!' finds its likeness in Arthur Nortje's poem titled 'At Rest from the Grim Place':

The sergeant laughs with strong teeth,
his jackboots nestle under the springbok horns.
Those bayonets are silent,
the spear of the nation gone to the ground.
I've seen the nebulae of a man's eyes
squirm with pain, he sang his life
through cosmic volleys. They call it
genital therapy, the blond bosses.[12]
(*Penguin*, 275)

The outrage at being discriminated against, the 'ill-mannered silence' that greets a black, even though he may be a Christian, is criticized vehemently by Maureen Watson in her poem, 'Memo to J.C.', and wryly by Wole Soyinka in his poem, 'Telephone Conversation'. Soyinka (Nigerian) writes, that when an African confesses his being black to a prospective landlady, he is encountered first by silence and then the query: "How Dark?...Are you light or very dark?" He is sickened by the "Stench/ Of rancid breath of public hide-and-speak". Eventually his pleading: "wouldn't you rather/ See for yourself?"[13] (*Ibid.*, 187) falls on deaf ears. Similarly Maureen Watson is bitter that though the Black Australians follow the "same basic" Christian values as "'sharin and carin' about each other", yet they are discriminated against:

> But they don't call us 'Followers of Jesus',
> They call us black fellas, man.[14] (Shoemaker, 269)

Such racial intolerance, stereotyping and stigmatizing, cut a deep wound in the sensibilities of both Aboriginal and African people, compelling each to arise and evoke:

> That spirit which asks no favour
> But to have dignity.[15] (*Penguin*, 78)

Much of the work by poets like Gerry Bostock, Lionel Fogarty, and Maureen Watson convey their dream and determination for an Aboriginal nation, as well as the aspiration to find their rightful place in the Australian society, while, at the same time, preserving the uniqueness and richness of their culture and customs. The little dilemmas which spotlight essential dissimilarities between Black and White Australians find a definitive voice in Aboriginal literature. Maureen Watson rues the fact, that though the Aboriginals live in their own land, they are, on the contrary, surrounded by a foreign race, making them foreigners in their own country. She strongly upholds her Aboriginal status with images such as:

> …the T-shirts that say 'I'm proud to be an Aborigine'…. 'I walk on Aboriginal Land'…so those images are coming. You know, we are holding up black mirrors for black reflections.[16] (Shoemaker, 278)

There is, however, a significant difference between black Australian literature and black African literature. The criticism and indictment of the white Australian, though loud and clear in Aboriginal literature, does not express the wish to drive them away. On the contrary, the sentiment most pronounced in African literature is the urge to drive away the white intruders. Ngudia Wendel of Angola in his poem, 'We Shall

Return, Luanda', advocates strongly, the desire of the people of Luanda, who wish to drive the white "murderers" away from their homeland, because they have "fed on the living body for ages/ like the bush tick"[17] (*Penguin*, 38-39). Oswald Mitshali, too, in 'The Birth of Shaka' declares with a ring of finalty:

Lo! You can kill me
but you'll never rule this land.[18] (*Ibid.*, 273)

Land represents for both, Aborigines and Africans, as indeed it does, for people the world over, an emotional connotation, which is much larger than its physical dimension. Land signifies inheritance, identity, a way of life, nurtured over generations and handed down from father to son. Les Murray in his poem titled, (a title which, incidentally, says it all) 'Thinking About Aboriginal Land Rights, I Visit the Farm I Will Not Inherit', writes:

By sundown it is dense dusk, all the tracks closing in.
I go into the earth near the hay shed for thousands of years.[19]
(Shoemaker, 199)

The white Australian merely owned the land, while the Aborigines belonged to it. Therefore their feeling of loss and sense of dispossession, as we can observe, is keen and deeply felt.

Racism, oppression, exploitation, dispossession and identity are some of the common themes that form the bulk of protest poetry, of both, Aboriginal and African literature. The whites were initially dismissive of this, but Black Australian literature gathered momentum because its history is a proud saga of resistance. Their rich oral culture which became accessible to the world only in the 1960s has since grown into a torrent, both in terms of output as well as readership. It has engendered a cultural nationalism for the maintenance and extension of Aboriginal pride and confidence.

Protest literature of the indigenous people of Africa shares a strong spiritual bond with Black Australian literature, because they too are oppressed 'first citizens'. These voices that can be heard from the dark, as they clamour for their traditions, land and resources, undoubtedly display an overriding sense of loss. There is no panacea for centuries of wrong and hurt, however, and the only way forward is a recourse to reconciliation and hope for a brighter future.

Oodgeroo Noonuccal herself earnestly wished for reconciliation. In her poem, 'Son of Mine', she tells Denis, her son, that she could tell him of heartbreak, of the brutal deeds that would shame mankind and fill him with hatred against those who perpetrated them. But she will not:

...I'll tell instead of brave and fine
When lives of black and white entwine
And men in brotherhood combine—
This I would tell you, son of mine.[20] (www.creativespirits.info)

In another poem, appropriately entitled, 'A Song of Hope', she entreats her people to leave the past behind and look towards a better future wherein a new Dreamtime would emerge. African poet Jean-Baptiste Tati-Loutard in his poem, 'Death and Rebirth' echoes in the same vein and exults:

I am at the Dawn of a people beginning a long march:
I shall see them break from their coop in all the sweat
Of their souls, as the sun breaks from the channels of the East
In a great transpiration of Light![21] (*Penguin*, 73)

The poet hopes to harness African aspirations to build a new country and to sing a new song. The silence of the Aborigine also turned into a strong resistance, as silence is often louder than words articulated with authority. Voices in the dark, having broken the silence, are now audible as they march towards a new dawn of hope and life. The binaries of domination and subordination, having thus been destabilized and re-defined, resistance and reconciliation become two sides of the same coin.

NOTES

1. Ngugi Wa Thiong'o, *Homecoming: Essays on African and Caribbean Literature, Culture and Politics,* Heinemann, London, 1972. xv.
2. 'The address given by his Holiness Pope John Paul II at the meeting with Aboriginal and Torres Strait Islander people at Alice Springs on 20 November, 1986', (Canberra, 1986) 4.
3. Gerald Moore and Ulli Beier, *The Penguin Book of Modern African Poetry.* Penguin Books Ltd.: Harmondsworth, U.K. 1986. 27.
4. *Ibid.*, 29.
5. Modern Australian Poetry (1901-1970), Australian Literature. MEG-09. IGNOU, New Delhi. 2002. 69.
6. *Ibid.*, 30.
7. *Ibid.*, 70.
8. *The Penguin Book of Modern African Poetry.* 70.
9. Adam Shoemaker, *Black Words White Page.* ANU E press. The Australian National University, Canberra. 2004. 265.

10. *Ibid.*, *Penguin*. 19.
11. *Ibid.*, Shoemaker. 270.
12. *Ibid.*, *Penguin*. 275.
13. *Ibid.*, 187.
14. *Ibid.*, Shoemaker. 269.
15. *Ibid.*, *Penguin*. 78.
16. *Ibid.*, Shoemaker. 278.
17. *Ibid.*, *Penguin*. 38-39.
18. *Ibid.*, 273.
19. *Ibid.*, Shoemaker. 199.
20. www.creativesprits.info/aboriginalculture/arts/aboriginalpoems
21. *Ibid.*, *Penguin*. 73.

WORKS CITED

Beier, Ulli, *Introduction to African Literature*. Longman Group Ltd.: Essex. 1982.

Fanon, Frantz, *The Wretched of the Earth*. Penguin Books Ltd.: Harmondsworth, U.K., 1969.

Gunew, Sneja, "Denaturalizing Cultural Nationalisms: Multicultural Readings of 'Australia'". *Nation and Narration*. Ed. Homi K. Bhabha. Routledge: New York. 2006.

IGNOU. Australian Literature (MEG- 09) *Modern Australian Poetry* (1901-1970).

Journal of Australian Studies. Special Issue. *Multiculturalism in Australian Literature* 1.

Moore, Gerald and Ulli Beier, Ed. *The Penguin Book of Modern African Poetry*. Penguin Books Ltd.: Harmondsworth, U.K. 1986.

Noonuccal, Oodgeroo, www.creativespirits.info/aboriginalculture/arts/aboriginalpoems.

Shoemaker, Adam, *Black Words White Page*. ANU E Press. The Australian National University, Canberra. 2004.

Soyinka, Wole, *A Shuttle in the Crypt*. Rex Collins Ltd. and Methuen London Ltd.: Wiltshire, U.K., 1986.

Taiwo, Oladele, *An Introduction to West African Literature*. Thomas Nelson and Sons Ltd., Lagos, 1985.

Thiong'o, Ngugi Wa, *Decolonizing the Mind*. James Currey Ltd.: London, 1986.

Walker, Kath, http://www.cit.griffith.edu.au//. 30 May, 2010.

Vintage Soul Searching for God: C.S. Singh's *Tapascharanam*

INDRAJEET MISHRA

MYSTICISM is to attain timelessness through time. Mysticism is a belief in a superior principle that vitalizes our life, thought, action and makes one feel the immortal reality emanating through the universe. It is a state of spiritual illumination, the rapturous delight and force that lets one have the realization of the ineffable being or absolute truth. Mystic beings encounter with infinite radiance and identify themselves with each and every living and non-living objects of the ambience. This idea of mysticism is closely allied with the transcendental, pantheistic and vedantic systems of life. In India myriad forms of mysticism is in practice. The yoga tradition believes in the realization of God through meditational process while devotional form of mysticism relies upon the unification of soul with almighty by surrendering mind and intellect completely. Patanjali has also propounded the idea of surrender of all actions to God. Eliade aptly observers, "In ancient and modern India, and indeed all through the East, we constantly find this strange mixture of 'difficult ways' and 'easy ways' of realizing mystical ecstasy or some other decisive experience" (Eliade as qtd. in Staal 97). Mysticism is a temper in which divinity emanates through matter. Its experiences are beyond time and space because eternal entity has no fixed structure as S.N. Dasgupta writes, "It is an ineffable, non-conceptual, inner experience, lying in its own unfathomable depth" (38).

Charu Sheel Singh, an Indian English poet well grounded in the philosophical and occult traditions of east and west both and his special areas of interest are Buddhism and theosophy, has structuralized his mystic experiences in *Tapascharanam* which contains 108 poems. The subliminal imagination carries the poet in a non-conceptual realm wherein he finds possibility of all kinds of potentialities. *Tapascharanam* is the joint venture of son Charu Sheel Singh and father Pratap Narain Singh as poet himself insists. It deals with the mythological character Sukhdev, the born enlightened son of Ved Vyas, who was reluctant to come out of mother's womb because of preconceived agony and difficulties of life. The collection is categorized as a Khand Kavya for perpetuating the great Indian epic tradition and total number of the poems has great numerological significance. The title of the poem suggests that poetry ensues from penance as Sukhdev is aggrieved at the gruesome aspects of the world. The collection is an epic venture hence it begins with the invocation to God:

Bring the pearl O God!
On the mythic geography
of linear constellations
and let the sea-shell
sing hymns primeval. (1)

Poet ardently appeals to God to bestow his blessing upon him for narrating the spiritual experiences. He tries to depict the reality of super-mental sphere that is neither exactly explainable nor understandable. However, for revelation and interpretation of the cocktail of creation one needs an eternal body of imagination. In the above quoted lines, pearl stands for poetic imagination and the creative fecundity of the poet. The unexplored and mythic geography he melts into figurative texture knitted into linguistical semantic. Krishna Banerjee has thrown light in the "Editorial" of the Triple Path on the basic modality of C.S. Singh's concentric imagination. She writes, "Everything begins and ends at the same point, be it the bindu, the navel of Vishnu or the egg of Brahma" (IX).

In chapter one *Adorations* poet admires and adores the creator of the universe. He finds himself caged in heaps of mud on the mortal realm but at the same time he realizes a stir within that makes him divine seeker. Like Medieval Bhakti poets Surdas, Meera, Kabir and Dadu, C.S. Singh has also devotional approach to God. Relationship between individual soul and God is that of groom and bride and bride in *Tapascharanam* is the transcendental being perpetually sought by the lover:

Seeking my bride in these
silent, sullen, empty areas
of the tombs of my identity
am I become old
in these realms of God.
O God! Come and make me
Thy companion soul. (3)

The groom and the bride echo Sankhya's prakriti and purush principle. One is the world as God, the other is its semantic component. In Shaiva literature, Shiva is Shaiva without the consort of Parvati who is shakti. The above quoted lines remind us of Tagore's *Geetanjali* where he feels:

> Thus it is that thy joy in me is so full thus it is that thou hast come down to me.
>
> O thou lord of all heavens, where would be thy love if I were not?
> Thou hast taken me as thy partner of all this wealth.
> In my heart is the endless play of thy delight
> In my life Thy will is ever taking shape. (42, Song No. 56)

Here the non-dualistic philosophy comes into play which has also been expressed by one of the most famous Hindi poets Kabir who states:

> Jal beech kumbh kumbh beech jal hai
> Futa kumbh jal jal hi samana.

Kabir has an identical experience and the awareness of time that he shows (Jal) is menacing and puzzling indeed. This makes Kabir go into the portfolios of Kumbh which is time yet beyond. In C.S. Singh's Mandala theory it is known as parabindu, the centre beyond the centre. Poet regards his soul as restless and dominated by worldly affairs in which fragrance of the long awaited divine presence is almost elapsed. He is in search of that poetic power which has been instrumental in making many a soul-stirring poems possible. Of course, that power is divine inspiration through which the poet wishes to achieve something worthwhile otherwise all his action is futile and insignificant. His approach to God resembles that of Tagore and Aurobindo who regard Him to be the source of all human achievements. Poet realizes sprouting of the sublime seed of thought that was hidden within him:

> The new petals of rose
> hide the secret of my soul.
> The budding leaves have brought out
> of a lifeless carnival,
> the song of celestial joy and immortal glory. (*Tapascharanam* 2)

The body is a conscious form of awareness of the extreme limitations it is exposed to. In yoga terminology one could say that a non-awareness of khestragya (knower of the field) leaves the body (khestra) alone deserted and desolate. Under such condition the human body is no different from the body of the animal. The quest of mystic in fact begins from here.

The body itself becomes the poem, rag, geet and ragazmakta. The body serves as a reflective mood of the soul, just as the soul is the ornament of the body, both of them are complete and complete each other, however, one is nitya (endless) and the other is anitya (permanent). In the human body soul resides hence both are important at their own place. It is human body that leads to spiritual realization. C.S. Singh realizes that this world is characterized by grizzly and sublime both. Most of the people in this world are treading on the demonic path of materialism. The allurement of matter is so irresistible that people have completely forsaken their spiritual side. In this world none seems to appreciate and acquire the meditational wisdom. Hence C.S. Singh like Tagore wishes to regenerate spirituality among people, he prays to God to wipe out all the deterrents from the path of spirituality. C.S. Singh like a true mystic feels the blazing glimmer of God's glory while enchanting His name. In the state of Dhyan he is encircled in the infinite circle in which the breath moves and the movement of breath is very rhythmical:

Moving circles of infinity
have encircled my total being
laying asleep my body I wander
in the infinite circles of glory
that are laid one over the other
for my soul to climb above the earth hoary. (4)

Similarly Sri Aurobindo in his poem 'Transformation' speaks as illumined soul. He is no longer a man of flesh and bone; he is transformed into God's happy tool. He raptures on the prospect of complete identity with the infinite. At the time of spiritual transformation one feels a peculiar rhythmic flow and the entire being becomes musical and ecstatic. To quote:

My breath runs in a subtle rhythmic stream
It fills my members with a might divine:
I have drunk the infinite like a giant's wine

Tapascharanam of C.S. Singh once again keeps forth significance of faith, prayer and meditation in the life of a mystic for searching his relationship with God. It is the process of meditation through which the bodily chakras can be broken and one can reach the state of Sat-chit-ananda. Meera refers to this as, "sooli upar sej piya ki/ kis bidh milna hoye". The soolis are actually the chakras and the divine figure resides above them so one needs to transcend these hurdles to meet God. Poetry becomes Moakshdayini when it is written out of Sadhana and manan.

The second chapter 'Glory of Nature' continues the journey of the soul in this world. Human soul is delighted to see the beautiful sublime painting of nature that God has painted with multiple hues and with different shape and size. The soul is mesmerized by beholding the, "milky, icy clouds, opal birds, trees and the meadows" (12) and it indulges in communion with the natural objects. Like an inquisitive child poet asks why you are so beautiful O cloud, and what melodious music you produce O springs? He realizes sameness and unity with the music produced out of rivulets.

> Thou art my Lord, ye regale my spirits;
> enraptured become I with joys divine
> silent objects commune to my quiet heart.
> I merrily dance forgetting the self,
> seer and the seen vanish
> I become one with God's creation. (*Tapascharanam* 13)

In the entire objects of nature energy is disseminated from one centre. Poet feels oneness with all of them. Krishna in *Bhagvatgeeta* states, "The whole cosmos is assimilated into me and I emanate through every object of the cosmos." As a matter of fact poets like Kabir, Wordsworth and many others have felt the presence of one Supreme power throughout the cosmos.

C.S. Singh being seer smiles at the ignorance of the people around him and thinks whether they will be able to "throw off their mask"? In the third Chapter, 'Mirage' he questions: will people of this world ever realize the deeper meaning of this life? There is always a misunderstanding between appearance and reality. What looks meaningful to us really has no meaning, and what is really meaningful is hardly perceived. The attempt of the poet to spiritualize the people continues:

> We live in houses
> whose masters we are not;
> we are dark phantoms
> struggling at least somewhere to get. (17)

Human life is ephemeral; our body is house and soul is the dweller as the time passes house gets ruined similarly human body gets tattered with the passage of time. In platonic view the whole world is mere appearance of reality and the same is known as Maya in Hindu scriptures. Buddhism also considers desire and charm of the unreal world as the cause of human misery. The duty of man is to understand the ephemerality of the mortal world and one must endeavor to redeem from the cycle of birth and rebirth. The concept of Mukti is propagated by the poet. C.S. Singh reveals his attachment to Almighty and wishes to be blessed by the company of God in secluded place where he sits for meditation. He makes an attempt to concentrate over the process of destruction and creation that is possible only with the utmost degree of imagination.

In *Agony* poet depicts the pang and darkness that soul faces living in the mortal world and in *Convulsion* climax of hopelessness and meaninglessness takes place in poet's journey of self-searching, moreover, his hope returns seeing the birds in a joyous mood singing the glory of God. It reminds him of His presence. The seeker realizes the path to reach Almighty is not straight rather full of mazes. It is like climbing the hill through a vertical way. However, it constantly makes a steady movement like an ant mounting a big mountain. After reaching the mountain the poet writes:

I looked not on Thee till I found
'You' and 'I' were a mental wall
I were bride and husband, one and all. (72)

World is operated from invisible force which we regard as God. In fact, God is an endless text and God is the real text, from where the cosmos emerges as a subtext and again loses its existence into the same. Here, the poet echoes Eliot's idea, "In my beginning my end lies." Our journey begins and ends on a point of time. The unison between the soul and Almighty takes place and micro soul merges into macro Reality. Thus, the quest gets completed and the wheel comes full circle. The soul arrives from where it has begun its journey. C.S. Singh beautifully depicts:

Into the navel of Brahma sinks the
threefold lotus and the meanings are implanted
there in the self's mental caves am I lost
for nothing neither comes nor goes anywhere. (73)

Buddhist suffering in Singh's poetry leads to the realization of Vedantic Brahma. In the Indian tradition the two have been in conflict with each other. In C.S. Singh one tradition leads to the other. One cannot conclude an article on mysticism. However, the frame of reference within which this article is written is a different time species. The time has come to a standstill and from this still centre of a moving world the carnival of life is glanced at from the vedantic, Buddhist, vedic, dualistic, non-dualistic and existential point of views. These secondary texts emanate out of my reading of *Tapascharanam*. There may be more I have not been able to decipher. As one enters into the collection one enters into the body of God and certain experiences are breath taking and self-consuming. Emanence here acquires the form of a personal relationship of God with the poet. Poet is not a person but paridrajaka, a persona with universal magnitude. The collection gives the impression that seed sprouts the syllable. The syllable becomes the logos. In the Western tradition God confused the speech of man at Tower, Bable. In the Indian tradition the speech itself becomes Rig Vedic Vak and the Vak set into the House of Being.

WORKS CITED

Aurobindo, Sri. *Savitri: A Legend and a Symbol*. Pondicherry: Sri Aurobindo Aashram Trust, 1993, Reprint.

_______. "Transformation" in *Indian Poetry in English*. Ed. Harimohan Prasad and Chakradhar Prasad Singh. New Delhi: Sterling Publishers Pvt. Ltd., 1997, Reprint.

Banerjee, Krishna. "Editorial" in *The Triple Path, Re-Inventing Poetic Genre: A Study of the Poetry of Charu Sheel Singh,* Vol I. Ed. Krishna Banerjee. New Delhi: Adhyayan Publishers and Distributors, 2007.

Dasgupta, S.N. *Hindu Mysticism*. Delhi: Motilal Banarsidass Pvt. Ltd., 2009, Reprint.

Singh, Charu Sheel. "Tapascharanam" in *Collected Poems*. New Delhi: Adhyayan Publishers and Distributors, 2008.

Stall, Frits. *Exploring Mysticism: A Methodological Essay*. Delhi: Motilal Banarsidass Pvt. Ltd., 2013.

Tagore, Rabindranath. "Gitanjali-Song Offerings" in An e-book Presentation by The Spiritual Bee. www.spiritualbee.com

Blended Boundaries of Fact and Fiction: Historicizing Kittur Through Literary Narration *The Queen of Kittur* by Dr. Basavaraj Naikar

SUMATHI SHIVAKUMAR

INTRODUCTION

POSTMODERN historical novels, regarded as historiographic metafictions, permit different voices and alternative, plural histories essentially by subverting the historical documents and events that they refer to. However, not all historical novels subvert history to give vent to the creative imagination of the writer. An actual record of historical facts in the form of a third person narrative can lend greater interest in the reader than archival material or a textbook with the same information. Such an historical narrative is usually written from the fictional character's point of view or perhaps as the story of a real person from history who has participated in the event. The novel, Queen of Kittur is a retelling of history from neither a contemporary of the event/times, nor an historian, but from the eyes of a creative writer, through the reconciliation of several binaries like historical objectivity vs nationalism, cultural present vs cultural history, historical facts vs literary imagination etc. What distinguishes a successful historical narrative from the rest is the presence of an engaging story without meddling with facts. Historiographic understanding of history forms the nucleus of this paper, claiming that it not only represents past events but unravels the underlying meaning in them as well. As a signifying system, therefore this narrative converts historical events into historical facts. The paper analyzes Basavaraj Naikar's *The Queen of Kittur* as an example of a historical narrative where the blending of fact and fiction is convincingly accomplished.

THE NARRATIVE AS HISTORIOGRAPHY

Historiography is the history of history. It can be a literary narrative that does not subject the actual events to historical analysis. Conversely, the subject of historiography is the record of the history of the event: the way it happened. It may, at times reflect conflicting objectives followed by different writers of different eras. Such differences arise more from perception of the times, rather than the events themselves. Therefore, such factors do influence the shaping of our understanding of the actual event, besides the nature of history itself.

Historiography, while constructing historical facts, selects certain past events and omits others, for ideological reasons. This reflects the fact that a select group is unintentionally denied an official voice by the dominant ideologies. Hence, history is relegated to being monologic, representing the dominant discourse and therefore as Orwell says, "History is written by winners." Hayden White, in "The Historical Text as Literary Artifact" vehemently argues that historians recreate history through "historical imagination." In other words the historian employs narrative strategies of a literary writer to convey his/her message. He coins the term "meta-history" which very succinctly blurs and sometimes blends the boundaries of facts and fiction. He further claims that history is essentially narrative prose, an amalgam of literary conventions and the historian's imagination. In the process, perhaps historical narrative can include types of "plots" or "emplotments" that include the tragic, comic, romantic, and satiric elements (Ricoeur, 31). Such an 'emplotment recalls Aristotle's claim that Poetry (Literature) tends to express the universal, history the particular. White questions the existence of the balance between factual reconstruction and imaginative recreation of the events. He probes into the "value neutral" aspect of retelling events. He endorses the need for examining fiction in history, a point raised by Orwell too.

As is clear from the above, it is possible to infer that the underlying attitude of historiography is one of skepticism. This stems from the belief that historians, particularly as writers do have agendas and do select sources with the intent of proving certain preconceived notions. History is, in this sense, never really objective, but is always deemed a construct that presents the historian-writer's perception of events or things. At its objective best—which is contestable—history (re)presents basic facts (dates, events, etc., as recorded in the available sources); the task on hand for the writer would be to interpret these supposed facts. This very interpretation, which, by definition a subjective mental process renders the product—a book, novel, etc., as less objective as possible.

Historiography permits foregrounding history as it unfolds in the literary narrative. Unlike historians, litterateurs do have the license to dwell deeper and unravel a profound historiographical insight. However, debatable its veracity may be, such insights help in forming a certain perspective about historical events. These are especially true in the case of colonialism when recordings were indeed one-sided and whose authenticity may be questioned. The natives somehow never really worried about serious documentation processes that have coerced both historians and literary writers to rely on the colonizers point of view.

THE STORY OF KITTUR: FACT VERSUS FICTION

The Queen of Kittur is a postmodern historical fiction that glorifies the heroism of the Rani, while combating both internal (Peshwa kings) and external (The East India Company, later day British colonizers) forces. The novel deals with the life of Rani Chennamma, the second wife of Raja Mallasarja of Kittur a small kingdom beaming with pride in tradition and culture.

The plot may be captured in a nutshell. Kittur, as a kingdom, is not overwhelmingly powerful in comparison to more prominent Mughals and many other neighbouring kingdoms. However, Raja Mallasarja has led the land with impeccable integrity, despite clandestinely escaping from the clutches of the Peshwas. His son Sivalingarudrasarja, not as able an administrator as his father, is issueless. Therefore, Rani Chennamma, decides to adopt a child—Sawai Mallasarja—from the village. As the king dies even before the formal adoption takes place, the ceremony is held before the final rites are performed for the king. This invites the attention of the British, as the 'Doctrine of Lapse', wherein, any king who dies without an heir to the throne forfeits the land to the British, had just come into effect. Thus begin the confrontation of the natives and the colonizers. The Queen sends emissaries with positive yet firm statements, refusing to give in to their demands. Notwithstanding the loss of Thackeray, two other generals and several others imprisoned, the British army repeatedly attacks Kittur. Displaying courage even in the face of defeat, the Rani symbolises 'shakti' in terms of female valor. Having tasted victory once, she is motivated to continue her confrontations with the British, consistently defying their orders. Her countrymen loved her audacious attitude and were highly supportive of her actions. Unfortunately for her and India, the internal feud and self-destructive betrayal by her own courtiers and the deceit and foul play on the part of the Company soldiers, ensure that the brave kingdom is brought to its knees. The ruthlessness of the colonizers, forces the helpless people to surrender. The valiant Queen is eventually imprisoned in the Fort of her own town, though the imperialists found it hard to subdue their admiration for her bravery. She dies in confinement.

THE STORY OF KITTUR'S HISTORY

Kittur's history is very much the story of Indian history, recorded in the view of the outsiders rather than the internal players. Several factors have influenced the course of documenting the history of this kingdom. Dearth of archival material, rigid imperialism during the Colonial regime that lasted for more than 300 years, a ravaging independence struggle that destroyed several human lives, lack of authentic documentation in the native language, and the eventual collapse of the kingdom have left the people of Kittur and India both powerless and speechless. Ignorance of English among the natives, and ignorance of Kannada or any other Indian language on the part of the British, rendered communication or a two-sided dialogue impossible between them. The conflicts within Kittur are of a varied nature and incomprehensible to the colonizers who lack an in-depth knowledge of the complexities within Indian cultural history. Lack of unity among the neighbouring kingdoms as they disagreed intensely on the issue of nationalism vs beneficial subordination, compounded the problems; thus making it extremely difficult for a collective fight. The failed attempt by the British to overawe the natives "by exhibiting the military wealth of the Company government" (Naikar, 168) resulting in the death of Thackeray himself reflects a total lack of understanding of the native strategising abilities, particularly in war. Such incidents forced the colonizers to resort to cunningness to conquer both lands and minds of India. Perhaps, this is the impetus for the author, Basavaraj Naikar to intensely preoccupy himself with the colonial past of India in this novel and reveal the richness of the Indian cultural history that encompasses the intellectual superiority of the people.

The novel projects loyalty, patriotism treachery of the natives and the scheming shrewdness of the British—the essential ingredients of an intriguing novel. It is this quality that demarks historical writing from literary writing.

The narrow divide between historical discourse and literary discourse, which, at times, is almost a slippage, as pointed out by Hayden White, is very relevant here. This enables reading the novel, primarily as a literary artist fictionalizing history solely for the sake of keeping Kittur alive and seeing it in books. In order to achieve this, he draws heavily from historical and quasi-historical sources for first-hand information. Such a method should provide an authentic historical dimension to his works.

Much of the action that is described in the novel is faithful to recorded history. Both in terms of dates and persons, the novel merely weaves the happenings into the narration. Some of the more easily accessible sources do mention the actual events as sequenced and presented in the novel. But the literary sources, mentioned at the beginning of the book give a clue to the role of imagination in effecting the narration in particular, the stringing of the different events. Starting from the first meeting of Raja Mallasarja and Chennamma as a brave girl capable of hunting and archery, their marriage, the rituals, their personal relationship, and many other socio-cultural revelations do carry colourful imagination. It is in these instances that the author's creative energy releases full steam.

The fascinating recreation, nevertheless offers the writer the choice of facts and the fictional element to interweave. It is only natural that writers conveniently omit certain facts to suit their contexts and perceptions. However, this novel transcends such methodical omission and presents history as 'it happened', with clear cut literary overtones. This novel can thus be described as a double-voiced discourse where, the people of Kittur, led by their Queen's impeccable authority and power, is subverted by the cunningness of the Company regiment. The dominant voice of imperialist eventually subverts the voices of the people. The author's expertise in blurring fact and fiction is at its creative best in these contexts.

The alternation of facts and fiction is seamless, and one needs an understanding the ethos of the land and its people to tell the difference between the political or historical clime from that of the cultural and social. For instance, the hurried coronation, with its intricate rituals are presented almost as a live coverage that we can see in the modern day televisions, though it is ostensibly true that the details could not have been recorded. It originates from the author's knowledge and understanding of the cultural milieu rather than extracting them from authentic sources. The songs sung during the wedding rituals of Chennamma and Raja Mallasarja is a classic case in point. This vindicates the intensity of the literary discourse as against the historical discourse.

Naikar provides a fictionalized history of Kittur in particular and India at large during crucial historical moments: the reign on Raja Mallasarja for nearly thirty-four years, (Naikar, 68), his meeting with

Bajirao Peshwa of Pune and the Raja's subsequent arrest and later his death, the controversial administration, illness and death of his son Sivalingarudrasarja, the 'quiet' but brave adoption of Sawai Mallasarja II, Rani Chennamma's war with Company regiment outside the fort of Kittur, the consequent arrest of Company Officers—Stevenson and Elliot, the democratic administration of the native Queen that earned the respect of the opponents, the eventual destruction of the Kittur palace and the death of the Queen.

Naikar's fictional space 'Kittur' is not an artistic construct born out of the narrator's imagination. It is the very embodiment of the first serious struggle for independence from foreign rule. He is intensely passionate with the history of Kittur and for posterity to have access to its recorded history as well. The urge to bring about the richness of Kittur's history is one of his foremost concerns, particularly when the nation's history seldom recognizes the Queen's prowess and patriotism. In contrast, Jhansi Rani Lakshmi Bai, who under very similar circumstances, defied the colonizers, apparently, is better known throughout the country. Writing, is Naikar's way of opening out to the outside world, at least to the present English speaking India, to become aware of the earliest instance of patriotic and anti-colonial wars. The novel yields very valuable insights into the complex and intricate history of Kittur. The need to fictionalize actual events is inevitable on the part of any writer living in politically distant times and conditions where writing is the only medium of expression. This is especially true at a time when we receive lies as truth, war as peace, and impoverishment as development. Under the circumstances, it's only just that a writer chooses, however unjustly, to offer truth camouflaged as fiction.

CONCLUSION

The general acceptance that popular history is something which we already know, or that the victors write/rewrite the history, does decimate the entire pursuit of history appreciably. However, a keen sense of historiography can intensify the writer's historical sense, thus enabling re-creation of history through a narrative. Establishing a rapport with the historical events through interrogation and interaction, will engage the writer more deeply with the historical events, may even necessitate consultation of additional sources to get the answers. It is precisely in this context that Basavaraj Naikar's *The Queen of Kittur* blends the boundaries that demark facts from fiction. The narration dovetails with the facts woven into literary imagination as is revealed by the historical events and socio-cultural activities. The ratio of facts and fiction can vary with each author and therefore the outcome may not comply with everyone's view of things. Nevertheless, it will allow a better appreciation for the many factors including, one's bias and prejudice, that contribute to the understanding and interpretation of an historical event. This appreciation, in turn, will enhance the quality of historical researches.

WORKS CITED

Aviezer, Tucker, ed. *A Companion to the Philosophy of History and Historiography*. Malden: Blackwell, 2009.

Hayden, White. "The Historical Text as Literary Artifact". Geoffrey Roberts. *The History and Narrative Reader*. Routledge; New York, 2001. 375-89 (452).

Iggers, Georg G. *Historiography in the 20th Century: From Scientific Objectivity to the Postmodern Challenge*. Wesleyan University Press: Connecticut, 2005.

Mittal, S.C. *India Distorted: A Study of British Historians on India*. M.D. Publications: New Delhi, 1995.

Naikar, Basavaraj. *The Queen of Kittur*. Kanva Publications: Bangaluru, 2012.

Orwell, Sonia and Ian Angus. *The Collected Essays*, Journalism and Letters of George Orwell. Secker & Warburg, 1968.

Ricoeur, Paul. *Time and Narrative*, Volume 1. Trans. Kathleen McLaughlin and David Pellaeur. University of Chicago Press: Chicago, 1984: 281.

Mnemonic Peregrinations and *The Shadow Lines*

PALLAVI SINGH

SO deeply shaken was the writer in him on witnessing the anti-Sikh communal riots in Delhi that followed in the wake of the assassination of the Indian Prime Minister Mrs. Indira Gandhi by her bodyguards in 1984, that decade later Amitav Ghosh wrote an essay entitled "The Ghosts of Mrs. Indira Gandhi": He admits that the episode was pivotal to his development as a writer as it informed his next novel *The Shadow Lines* and its successor *In An Antique Land.*

In *The Shadow Lines* Amitav Ghosh employs a narrative in which time and space is fluid. It is constantly shifting from one location to another, from one moment to another without any forced transition, like the ebb and flow of thoughts taken out of memory which are at once both personal and subjective. It struggles to define a difficult trauma, which though being personal and subjective, intersects with larger historical forces and public events.

An unnamed first person narrator, through whose consciousness everything that happens in the course of the narrative is mediated, recalls his boyhood admiration of his uncle Tridib. His death in a communal riots is the pivot around which the narrator's mnemonic peregrinations revolve. The narrator, however was not present at Tridib's death so his attempt to make sense of it is haunted by this absence. Around this nucleus, the narrator's swirl of memories is constructed through the accumulation of other people's recollections of the event: Tridib's younger brother, Robi and May Price, an English woman with whom Tridib was becoming romantically involved. It is through their narratives that his own is assembled and the novel discloses how an identity is patched up—or woven, through inter-connecting narratives which may or may not add up to something.

Even at the end of the novel, the narrator is still, to all intents and purposes, at a loss to explain what happened to Tridib. In an effort to locate the cause of his uncle's murder in a communal riot, the narrator realizes a historical quest on trying to explain another 'absence', the silence about the riot in the national records, the national media, and consequently its absence in the narrator's own memory. He realized that in order to maintain a coherent sense of individual identity traumas might be repressed by individuals. In the same way as collective identities repress those things which disturb their self-image, those events that might fragment the coherence of the larger narratives of history, nation and state.

The shadow lines of the title are, therefore, both subjective and objective, experiential as well as political. They are symbolically those invisible lines that demarcate the transition from youth to maturity, the past from the present. They are those intangible but indelible markers that identify oneself from others, ones own 'community' from others. The material borders of political entities such as nations or states which physically mark and limit the spatial and temporal coordinates of their citizens' experiences. In its form, however, the novel also enacts the transgression of these shadow lines, moving across space and time with an ease that challenges the permanence that political borders aspire to represent.

The novel takes place mostly on the newly created Indo-Pakistan border. It largely includes three generations of narrators family, dispersed over East Bengal, Calcutta and London. It was in 1960's in Calcutta that the novel opens, and portrays two families—one English, one Bengali—familiar to each other since the time of the Raj, as their lives intermingle in a tragic and comic manner. The unnamed narrator travels between Calcutta and London in 1981 to tell the story which contains multiple stories of his grandmother Th'amma, and his grandaunt Mayadebi, of his uncles Tridib and Robi, of his cousins Ila, and of May Price, a family friend in London. All these overlapping stories are united by the thread of memory, as the novelist treats memory as a driving force of the narrative.

While going down the memory lane the narrator tries to inhabit a transnational space like Tridib to achieve freedom and liberty in its entirety since freedom is quite central to every characters story in the novel. Since, he continuously contests with artificial divisions of the subcontinent as well as "colonial or postcolonial" cartographies, the novel attempt to present the transnational space through the imagination of the narrator and his most influential relative Tridib. This space is addressed not only as a space of human and cultural encounters, but of overlapping histories and territories, shifting countries and continents where different people, cultures, nations and communities communicate above the "shadow lines" of social, national and territorial barriers. However, the idea of transnational space in the novel presents the role of national ideologies in shaping personal memory and collective history.

A number of instances of memory and imagination at work, by most of the characters could be observed, while going through the novel—such as —telling stories and events, evoking the role of imaginary and real places across distant cultures and communities, watching fading photographs, reading maps and old newspapers, reminiscing about forgotten episodes of mutual bonding and playing childhood games. The unnamed narrator confesses that he has learned the practice of imagining space and place from his alter-ego Tridib. The narrator reveals that, it is Tridib who has given him "world to travel" and "eyes to see them with" (*SL*, 20)[1].

The narrator confesses that it is Tridib who had created in him a longing to imagine familiar and unfamiliar places in memory and imagination. Both the narrator and Tridib are often found in the novel studying maps to develop and discover their distinct sense of travelling to different places without any kind of mental and physical border or barrier. Tridib as such triggers in the narrator a desire to travel around the globe and even suggests the narrator to use his 'imagination with precision' (*SL*, 24) in order to voyage around unknown spaces. He once said to him that one could never know anything except through desire "that carried one beyond the limits of one's mind to other times and other places, and even, if one was lucky, to a place where there was no border between oneself and one's image in the mirror" (*SL*, 29).

The narrator feels sad for his cousin Ila, who has no concept of place because she could not invent a place for herself rather she relies on the inventions of others:

> I could not persuade her that place does not merely exist, that it has to be invented in one's imagination; that her practical, bustling London was no less invented than mine, neither more nor less true, only very far apart. It was not her fault that she could not understand, for as Tridib often said to her, the inventions she lived in moved with her, so that although she had lived in many places, she had never travelled at all. (*SL*, 21)

Throughout the novel, we find Ila considering space only as a given reality, she is never found to believe in space as a human construction. Ila never makes an attempt to understand the narrator as well, rather she dismisses his indulgence with imaginary space construction as a mere indulgence in fancy:

> It's you who were peculiar, sitting in that poky little flat in Calcutta, dreaming about faraway places. I probably did you no end of good; at least you learnt that those cities you saw on maps were real places, not like those fairylands Tridib made for you. (*SL*, 23-24)

The narrator realizes that Ila is trapped in a static zone, although she has travelled throughout the globe. The reason behind Ila's static mentality could be that she is unable to see any affinity between the past and present especially when memory is not crucial to her conception of space and place. Ila is unable to see the past through memory or imagination whereas once the narrator has seen the past through Tridib's eyes, the past "seemed concurrent with its present" (*SL*, 31). The narrator illustrates:

> Ila lived so intensely in the present that she would not have believed that there really were people like Tridib, who could experience the world as concretely in their imagination as she did through her senses, more so if anything, since to them these experiences were permanently available in their memories. (*SL*, 29-30)

Although Ila wants to enjoy a sense of bonding with the narrator, she at the same time humiliates him for living in such a lowly place like Calcutta and Delhi where no events of global importance ever take place, "nothing that sets a political example to the world, nothing that's really remembered" (*SL*, 102). Ila's mentality confuses the narrator, for whom the whole world seems to be a mosaic of interconnected places. Calcutta for him is as much a part of London as London is a part of Calcutta, especially when all places seem to be borderless spaces in the process of memory. He seems to be astonished to see that Ila has no understanding of events outside the colonial motherland England:

> I began to marvel at the easy arrogance with which she believed that her experience could encompass other moments simply because it had come later; that times and places are the same because they happen to look alike, like airport lounges. (*SL*, 101)

He emphasizes that many events of global importance might have occurred in London but this does not mean that the sacrifices and sufferings of our own countrymen during the political calamities of sixties and seventies as well as in history should be—sniggered at. He considers England only as a homeland of imagination, maintaining, "I knew nothing at all about England except an invention. But still I had known people of my own age who had survived the Great Terror in the Calcutta of the sixties and seventies (*SL*, 103).

The narrator is seen time and again in the novel using the idea of memory and imagination in "inventing places", because he wants to comprehend space beyond any spatial borders. As a school boy, the pictures of London he conjured were so vivid that he could recognize the places by the mere mention of their names when he visited London years later and learned that real places can be invented inside your head:

> the Tridib who had pushed me to imagine the roofs of Colombo for myself, the Tribid who had said that we could not see without inventing what we saw, so at least we could try to do it properly.... Because...if we didn't try ourselves, we would never be free of other people's inventions. (*SL*, 31)

The narrator further edifies the relationship of Tridib and May as the most awe-inspiring experience in his memory because their vision of love and bonding is not constricted by either national fervour or racial hatred. In keeping with this idea, Tridib had expressed in his last letter to May that he wanted them to "meet far away from friends and relatives—in a place without a past, without history, free, really free, two people coming together with the utter freedom of strangers" (*SL*, 141).

In fact, Tridib epitomises the narrator's as well as every other character's desire to overcome the "shadow lines" of borders and distance to inhabit a space of cultural and human contact.

The narrator proceeds to delve into the past portraying a series of political incidents in Calcutta and Dhaka simultaneously. Out of the many incidents, the incident which stands out to be "branded in [the narrator's] memory" (*SL*, 222) is the one in which Tridib had lost his life. While recollecting an individual's sacrifice and his community's struggle with senseless political and national barriers, the narrator states:

> Every word I write about those events of 1964 is the product of a struggle with silence. It is a struggle I am destined to lose—have already lost—for even after all these years I do not know where within me, in which corner of my world, this silence lies. All I know of it is what it is not. It is not, for example, the silence of an imperfect memory. Now is it a silence enforced by a ruthless state—nothing like that: no barbed wire, no check points to tell me where its boundaries lie. (*SL*, 213)

It is in 1979 that the narrator is seen to recollect the events of 1964, because he is determined not to let "the past vanish without trace; I was determined to persuade them of its importance" (*SL*, 271).

The narrator uses memory not only to present something that has been confounding him for fifteen long years, but also to figure out "what" and "how" to remember. Hence may be this is the reason why the narrative reflects a constant process of introspection; as Louis James proclaims, "if *Circle of Reason* is about knowledge, *The Shadow Lines* is about knowing" (56).[2]

The novel does not only present the descriptions of the riots of 1964 and the loss of life by innocent people but it also presents a tribute to someone who had dreamed of a borderless subcontinent. The narrator recollects:

> by the end of January 1964 the riots had faded away from the pages of the newspapers, disappeared from the collective imagination of "responsible opinion", vanished without leaving a trace in the histories and bookshelves. They had dropped out of memory into the crater of a volcano of silence. (*SL*, 226)

The narrator while reading the old newspapers in his study finds out that the riots in Khulna and Calcutta have not ever made the newspaper headlines, but became a mere bottom page story. At this stage, the narrator has started the "strangest journey: a voyage into a land outside space, an expanse without distances; a land of looking-glass events" (*SL*, 219). The narrator gets deeply disturbed at this realisation that a distance of twelve hundred miles between Srinagar (Kashmir) and Calcutta, and "Dhaka being in another country", could be used as a reason to keep people in Calcutta in the dark. This realisation makes the narrator discover a momentous truth that, national frontiers create a false sense of distance and reality that they create a false illusion of differences.

The narrator also describes about the communal riot of Dhaka and its consequent effect of the poisoning of the water in Calcutta in 1964, by Muslims. The narrator felt at that time that "our city had turned against us" (*SL*, 199). The terror of riot was so intense that he could not even trust his Muslim friend, Montu and he remembers fear suddenly filling the familiar space of his native city:

> It is a fear that comes of the knowledge that normally is utterly contingent, that the spaces that surround one, the streets that one

> inhabits, can become, suddenly and without warning, as hostile as a desert in a flash flood. It is this that sets apart the thousand million people who inhabit the subcontinent from the rest of the world—not language, not food, not music—it is the special quality of loneliness that grows out of the fear of the war between oneself and one's image in the mirror. (*SL*, 200)

However, in the novel we also meet grandmother's orthodox Hindu uncle Jethamoshai, who had never let the shadow of any Muslim ever pass him all his life, but after the partition when he has almost lost his senses, he is happily looked after by a Muslim family. He comments that his fate is tied up with his land whether his land is transferred to his enemies or not:

> Once you start moving you never stop. That's what I told my sons when they took the trains. I said: I don't believe in this India-Shindia. It's very well, you're going away now, but suppose when you get there they decide to draw another line somewhere? What will you do then? Where will you move to? No one will have you anywhere. As for me; I was born here, and I'll die here. (*SL*, 211)

The interconnectedness between space and individual memory and collective history, the novel depicts how nationalism invades private lives and how political histories shape personal memories. The novel as such shows how nationalism invades our lives, whether we fight it or not and how it determines human relationships. While commenting on Ghosh's logic of drafting the politics of space in the novel, Mukherjee makes a pertinent comment:

> Amitav Ghosh would like to believe in a world where there is nothing in between, where borders are illusions. Actually three countries get interlocked in Amitav Ghosh's *Shadow Lines*—East Pakistan before it became Bangladesh, England, and India—and people of at least three religions and nationalities impinge upon one another's lives and deaths. It is a text of our times when human lives spill over from one country to another, where language and loyalties cannot be contained within tidy national frontiers. (181)[3]

Both the narrator and Tridib as a historian and archaeologist respectively, complement each other in the novel as a narrative of memory. The narrator admits that even years after his death, Tridib seems to be watching over him as he tries:

> to learn the meaning of distance. His Euclidean space, Chiang Mai in Thailand was much nearer Calcutta that Delhi. (*SL*, 227)

Thus, time and distance like space and place appear to be a mystery that the narrator has to reckon with to relive his dying past. Due to a long silence within and without with respect to the individual and communal crisis of 1964, it takes the narrator "fifteen years to discover" that there was a connection between the "nightmare bus ride back from school and the events that befell Tridib and others in Dhaka" (*SL*, 214). The narrator feels stupid on realizing the truth, so late in his life:

> I believed in the reality of space; I believed that distance separates, that it is a corporeal substance; I believed in the reality of nations and borders; I believed that across the border there existed another reality.... I could not have perceived that there was something more that an incidental connection between those events of which I had a brief glimpse from the windows of that bus, in Calcutta and those other events in Dhaka, simply because Dhaka was in another country. (*SL*, 214)

Despite condemning the masses' obsession with the "shadow lines" of hatred and hostility out of national sentiments, the narrator also shows how ordinary people try their best to seek mutual sympathy among various ethnic groups of the subcontinent. Evidences can be drawn in both the cases, firstly during the partition of the country and later on during the trouble in Dhaka in 1964, there were innumerable cases of Muslims in East Pakistan giving shelter to Hindus and Hindus sheltering Muslims. "But they were ordinary people, soon forgotten—not for them any Marty's Memorials or Eternal Flames" (*SL*, 225). However, the narrator tries to bring out the mentality of ordinary people through the grandmother who believes in drawing lines not only as a part of her faith but also respecting them with blood. The narrator eventually arrives at the conclusion that "there was a special enchantment in lines" (*SL*, 228) as the pattern of the world. Hence, ordinary people are enchanted with borders, with "imagined communities"[4] no matter how much of "an invented tradition"[5] these borders and imagined communities are. The narrator concludes:

> They had drawn their borders, believing in that pattern, in the enchantment of lines, hoping perhaps that once they had etched their borders upon the map, the two bits of land would sail away from each other like the shifting tectonic plates of the prehistoric Gondwanaland,

> what had they felt, I wondered, when they discovered that they had created not a separation, but a yet—undiscovered irony—the irony that killed Tridib. (*SL*, 228)

The narrator attempts to present his profound association with Tridib who is an embodiment of freedom and suggests both space and place as subject to divisions and differences where there should be no border or barrier. The narrator tries to demonstrate the irony of his relatives sacrifice. He highlights that Tridib as a staunch believer of inventing and producing a transnational space gave his life away to save human lives, but the borders stayed where they were.

The two subtitles of the novel, 'coming home' and 'going away' refer to the dilemma of space and place for the people of contemporary India, Pakistan and Bangladesh. The narrator explains that the dogmatic Indian nationalists are obsessed with drawing lines and shutting doors on each other when in history they were all one people. "Going away" and "Coming Home" was something one could easily achieve without risking one's life in the subcontinent; as for moving from Dhaka to Calcutta and vice-versa, people were not supposed to show any identity proof as passport in the past. Ghosh states:

> the simple fact that there had never been a moment in the four-thousand-year-old history of that map, where the places we know as Dhaka and Calcutta were more closely bound to each other than after they had drawn their lines—so closely that I, in Calcutta, had only to look into the mirror to be in Dhaka; a moment when each city was the invented image of the other locked into an irreversible symmetry by the line that was to set us free—our looking glass border. (*SL*, 228)

The narrative attempts to shed down the imagined differences between the newly created nation states on the subcontinent by emphasizing similarities between Dhaka and Calcutta, by using the term 'mirror'. He further suggests that both these nations have "looking glass border" which only suggests a mirage of otherness but actually sees itself reflected. Once while experimenting with a compass on Tridib's old atlas, the narrator suggests that even though he 'believed in the power of distance' (*SL*, 222) he could not help ignoring that Calcutta and Khulna, despite being separated by national barriers "face each other at a watchful equidistance across the border" (*SL*, 226). As such, he is convinced that "border", are mere "shadows" of the mind.

The narrator's grandmother is possessed of a primordial view of nationalism and equates native space with freedom and honour in an era when the question of national identity has undergone radical changes. She states that Ila has no right to stay in England as she is not a "national" of that place. Th'amma questions furiously, "what's she doing in that country?" (*SL*, 76) and reasons out:

> She doesn't belong there. It took those people a long time to build that country; hundreds of years, years and years of war and bloodshed.... War is their religion. That's what it takes to make a country. Once that happens people forget they were born this or that, Muslims or Hindu, Bengali or Punjabi: they become a family born of the same pool of blood. That is what you have to achieve for India, don't you see? (*SL*, 76)

After her retirement in 1962 as a headmistress from a public school, she feels a profound sense of nostalgia for her birth-place in Dhaka. She sadly recollects that her ancestral house was partitioned with a wall between two brothers, her father and her uncle, Jethmoshai. The readers first encounter the partition of domestic space, a partition that is again presented by the partition of the national space with the partition of the subcontinent in 1947. The grandmother seems to be aware of the reality of the border, she questions her son whether she will be able to see "the border between India and East Pakistan, from the plane," (*SL*, 151) during her visit to Dhaka or not. At the response of her son who challenges her definition of nationalism Th'amma further states:

> But if there aren't any trencher or anything, how are people to know? I mean, where's the difference then? And if there's no difference, both sides will be the same; it'll be just like it used to be before, when we used to catch a train in Dhaka and get off in Calcutta the next day without anybody stopping us. What was it for all then—the partition and the killing and everything—if there isn't something in between? (*SL*, 151)

When Robi tries to recollect Tridib's death, while in a restaurant in England, fifteen years after his death, he expresses bitterly the cynicism towards the new nation states which is seminal to Ghosh's view of the present-day subcontinent:

> And then I think to myself, why don't they draw thousands of little lines through the whole subcontinent and give every little place a new name? What would it change? It's a mirage; the whole thing is

> a mirage. How can anyone divide memory? If freedom was possible, surely Tridib's death would have set me free. (*SL*, 241)

By recollecting the events of 1964 and their role in shaping private and public spaces, Ghosh gives a new perspective on personal and historical memory. Even the development of the story "becomes a commentary on the ways in which histories get constructed" (Singh, 163).[6] As has been noted by Brinda Bose:

> Ghosh's fiction takes upon itself the responsibility of re-assessing its troubled antecedents, using history as a tool by which we can to begin to make sense of—or at least come to terms with—our troubling present. (235)[7]

As the story moves forward, the strands of memory, history, space and nation are woven into each other, to present an overlapping family chronicles. Bose further adds:

> As the narrator in *The Shadow Lines* embarks upon a journey of discovery of roots and reasons, the more of the one he unearths leaves him with loss of the other. He is forced to conclude that knowing the causes and effects of that history which he had not fully apprehended as a child was not an end in itself. The metajourney that this novel undertakes follows the narrator—as he weaves and winds his way through a succession of one—imaginary homelands—into that third space where boundaries are blurred and cultures collide, creating at once a disabling confusion and an enabling complexity. No story—or history, for that matter—can be acceptable as the ultimate truth, since truths vary according to perspectives and locations. (239)[8]

For Ghosh, indeed for most Indians the term 'partition' carries resonances that extend beyond its literal meaning. It invokes memories of the catastrophic events that accompanied the 1947 Partition of the Indian subcontinent into two nations—India and Pakistan. The resulting triangle of associations between 'religion', 'nationalism' and 'partition' has its source and motivation in anxieties generated by the politics of identity in the Indian subcontinent. *The Shadow Lines* represents Ghosh's most direct confrontation with nationalism and national identity. It is unsurprising, therefore, that the motif of the map appears throughout the novel—the Barthalomew Atlas, the floor plans of houses, real or imagined. On discovering the connection between his uncles Tridib's death and the riots he had been caught up in as a child, the narrator picks up his Bartholomew Atlas and with the aid of a 'rusty old compass' draws geometrical circles that distance is as much a figurative concept as it is a physical one. "What distances Chiang Mai or Chengdu from Calcutta is not their geographical proximity or otherwise to Calcutta but rather their location outside the mental map of the nation-state and the borders that demarcate its space from that of its neighbours."[9]

Nations, therefore, are a mental construct, a space imagined much more than a portion of earth, surrounded by borders containing within them people to whom the nation belongs. People who may not have seen other, living thousands of miles apart, yet sharing an identity, a similarity because of a "silent communion of their minds".[10]

Nations are, therefore, both 'real' as well as 'imaginary'. This is precisely why Ghosh suggests that the borders that separate them are 'shadow lines'. The novel illustrates this by expressing the nationalist literal mindedness of the narrator's grandmother who 'wanted to know whether she would be able to see the border between India and East Pakistan from the plane'. "It doesn't matter whether we recognize each other or not. We're the same flesh, the same blood, the same bone, and now at last, after all these years, perhaps we'll be able to make amends for all that bitterness and hatred"[11] (*SL*, 142).

The map upon which the nation is inscribed is, like a text, merely a representation of the world, a metaphor of space itself. The location of its borders may not necessarily coincide with the imagined community that is brought into being through the language of nationhood. This becomes the cause of perplexity to the grandmother who cannot comprehend how her place of birth had come to be so messily at odds with her nationality. In a moment of lucidity both Th'amma and the senile Jethamoshai echo the same sentiments as they contemplate the implications of the arbitrariness of borders.

REFERENCES

1. Ghosh, Amitav, *The Shadow Lines* (1988). New York: Houghton Mifflin, 2005: 20. All subsequent references are to this edition and appear in parentheses in the article.
2. James, Louis, "*Shadow Lines*: Cross-Cultural Perspectives in the Fiction of Amitav Ghosh." *The Novels of Amitav Ghosh.* Ed. R.K. Dhawan. New Delhi: Sangam, 1999: 52-58.
3. Mukherjee, Meenakshi, *Elusive Terrain: Cultural and Literary Memory.* New Delhi: Oxford UP, 2008: 181.

4. Anderson, Benedict, *Imagined Communities: Reflections on the Origin and Spread of Nationalism.* London: Verso, 1983: 15.
5. Hobsbwam, Eric and Terence Ranger, Eds., "Introduction: Inventing Tradition." *The Invention of Tradition.* Cambridge: Cambridge UP, 2000: 1-14.
6. Singh, Sujala, "The Routes of National Identity in Amitav Ghosh's *The Shadow Lines.*" *Alternative Indias: Writing, Nation and Communalism.* Eds. Peter Morey and Alex Tickell. Amsterdam: Rodopi, 2005: (161-80).
7. Bose, Brinda, "Footnoting History: The Diasporic Imagination of Amitav Ghosh." In *Diaspora: Theories, Histories, Texts.* Ed. Makarand Paranjape. New Delhi: Indialog, 2002: 235-45.
8. *Ibid.*, 239.
9. Mondal, Anshuman A., *Amitav Ghosh.* Delhi: Viva Books, 2010: 87.
10. Kumar, Deepak, *Science and the Raj: 1857-1905*, New Delhi: Oxford University Press, 1997: 67.
11. Ghosh, Amitav, *The Shadow Lines,* New Delhi, Penguin/Viking, 2008: 142.

Faith and Conglomerate Ideas in the Poetry of Swami Vivekananda

MAHIMA SINGH

Ye yatha mam prapadyante
tamstathaiva bhajamyahum
mama vartmanuvartante
manusyah partha sarvasah. (*Gita*: Chapter 4 Verse No. 11)

VIVEKANANDA is decidedly a key figure in ushering the cultural renaissance in India in the 19th century. He also re-interpreted *Vedanta* in terms of a rationalistic thought structure which did not carry the metaphysical burdens. The quotation from *The Bhagavatgita* establishes the foundation upon which Vivekananda erected his pillars of faith consider the following lines from Vivekananda *Chicago Addresses*:

> The Christian is not to become a Hindu or a Buddhist, nor a Hindu or a Buddhist to become a Christian. But each must assimilate the spirit of the others and yet preserve his individuality and grow according to his own law of growth. (60)

The above statement by Vivekananda is possibly the best interpretation of the verse from *The Bhagavatgita* (Chapter 4 Verse No. 11). The founding principles of Vivekananda's religion of faith were fairly simple: human beings are not to be substituted by rituals, dogmas, other unnecessary paraphernalia that accompanies religious practices all over the world. In his inspired moments Vivekananda wrote the following lines of the poem entitled "In Search of God":

> All creeds do come from Thee;
> The Vedas, Bible, and Koran bold
> Sing Thee in harmony. (*In Search of God and Other Poems* 5)

Vivekananda's faith in functional God is evident enough; the truth is that Vivekananda continues the tradition of medieval same poetry with an intellectual rigour that was not available before. This paper is therefore justifiably focusing upon Vivekananda's poetic talent which now deserves recognition that has been due for a long time.

Vivekananda's poetry is self-exhortation, self-deconstruction in and by the same argument, self-creative to his poetry was a kind of uprise, and uplifting into one's subliminal self. His poetry time and again tells us that religion is not a form of institution; it is a form of living considers the following poems entitled "The Living God":

> He who is at once the high and low,
> The sinner and the Saint,
> Both God and worm,
> Him worship—Visible, Knowable, real, omnipresent,
> Break all other idols! (*In Search of God and Other Poems* 20)

It is Significant to note that Vivekananda's belief in an omnipresent God still sustains it is realistic flavor. He has no faith in evolving thousands of Gods and Goddesses. One God is enough as the point of origination and the source of all our idealistic fulfillment. For more than a belief in an invisible god, Vivekananda believed in the might of the materiality of man which has always created a God in all cultural cycles: Vivekananda said in his *Chicago Addresses* "Every religion is only evolving a God out of the material man, and the same God is the inspirer of all of them" (46).

As pointed out earlier Vivekananda reinterpreted Vedanta in a more realistic manner unlike Aadi Shankeracharya who had an idealistic and metaphysical touch in his interpretation as contains with the *Brahamsutra.* Vivekananda thus spoke in one of his *Chicago Addresses*:

> I am proud to belong to a religion which has taught the world both tolerance and universal acceptance. We believe not only in universal toleration, but we accept all religions as true. (20)

Here, Vivekananda outlines the essential tenets of all religion particularly Hinduism. Hinduism believes in all kind of religious practices as other religion have expounded; however Hinduism also believes that universal brotherhood and tolerance are the precious ornaments all religion should possess. Obviously Vivekananda is hitting at those religions which have got proselytizing zeal which is less concern with human beings as human beings and more concern with human beings as Muslim and Christian and the rest.

Aadi Shankeracharya's interpretation of Vedic and Upanishadic tradition is not man-centred; Vivekananda established a human relevance to vedantic teachings. The tradition of medieval saint poetry similarly is searching for God, not always within the human breast but in an imperceptible space which cannot fully articulated. Medieval saint poetry therefore is theistic as well as dualistic:

> In temple, church and mosque,
> In vedas, Bible, Al Koran
> I had rearched for Thee in vain. (*In Search of God and Other Poems* 3)

And further in "No One to Blame":

> I am my own embodied past;
> Therein the plan was made;
> The will, the thought, to that confirm,
> To that the outer frame;
> No one but me to blame. (*In Search of God and Other Poems* 12)

The first lines from the poem of Vivekananda disorients the thought of bookish religion in shining God within the nerves and arteries of living what are the *Vedas, Koran* and the *Bible.* If they do not generate love, tolerance, universal brotherhood within me.

This is clearly Vivekananda's faith not in hypothetical God but in a living one—a God who enjoys his immanence in the multiple variety of this world. Vivekananda is also unlike Walt Whitman who says that time and place do not matter. For Vivekananda time and place are forms of God and appearances too, which are the decorations God puts upon himself. In an important poem called "One More Circle" *Chicago Addresses* Vivekananda expresses an identical idea: "Threads of life—Spins out a stronger piece" (*In Search of God and Other Poems* 34).

Vivekananda as a true renaissance intellectual thought that Buddhism offers a meta critique of Hinduism. Just as Buddha rejuvenated Hinduism during his lifetime, Vivekananda sustains Hinduism in his arm way during his lifetime. There is a lot of justification thinking as Vivekananda did that Buddhism fulfills the ideals Hinduism chariot for along. Buddha re-centered faith in the human being himself and not in novo-daddy God who resided outside the circle of human reason. Buddha similarly castigated like Vivekananda empty ritualism and meaningless idol worship. Vivekananda is not really same that Buddhist *shunya* is a symbol of agnosticism; on the contrary; he is linking the great *shunya* tradition with a functional god who is within us all, and a more so in *Daridra Naryan* who need to be fore-grounded in the Indian social set up. This effort by Vivekananda can be compared by the efforts of Gandhi and Aurobindo in their ways, began uplifting the lots of the downtrodden people by starting the journals called the *Harizan* and the *Arya*. Vivekananda provides Vedanta a radical shift in emphasis and that shift is so close to the *karmyoga* of *The Bhagavadgita*. Karma is the religion and man is an article of faith. Consider these lines from *Chicago Addresses*:

> ...the agnosticism of the Buddhists, and the atheism of the Jains, each and all have a place in Hindu Religion. (26)

This amply exhibits that evil, agnosticism, atheism and the rest of the form of the believe lead only to God.

For Vivekananda, it is interesting to note, nationalism itself is a form of religion. This religion is assimilative in intend and native and does not nourish ill-will, jealousy or hatred towards other nation. Time and again Swamiji said that a better Hindu would always make a better Christian or better Muslim. Similarly a better Christian all for that matter, a better Muslim, would make a better Hindu. That is really the essence of religion according to Vivekananda consider the following poem from the poem "Light".

> I look behind and after
> And find that all is right,
> In my deepest sorrows
> There is a soul of light. (*In Search of God and Other Poems* 34)

Religion as the poem says is an enlightening experience: it transcends limiting structure of consequences that disintegrate and bring about a break in the integral approach. The point has been made earlier that Vivekananda did away with useless dogma, ritual and useless paraphernalia. The means that Vivekananda religion is founded upon the universalism ingrained in the seminal concepts of all religions: He spoke in *Colombo to Almora*:

> If you are a real lover of Shiva, you must see Him in everything and in everyone. You must see that every worship is given unto Him whatever may be the name or the form; that all knees bending toward the Caaba, or kneeling in a Christian church, or in a Buddhist temple are kneeling to Him whether they know it or not,.... He is the one lord of all, the one Soul of all souls. (15)

What is evident here is swamiji's yogic method which always separated the chaff from the grain. Earlier Edmund Husserl had propounded his phenomenological theory by constituting two kinds of reductions eidetic and transcendental. This was Husserl way of discovering universals within the particular. Vivekananda thought that nationalism is not necessarily a geographical entity; for him it was a spiritual space. The truth is that the idea of vasudhaiva kutubhkam—"The whole world is my family"—is founded upon this universalism only. The nation is a narration and the narration makes no distinction between this and that because it's germinating power is love which founds universal brotherhood. In "To a Friend" he writes:

> Love, love—that's the one thing,
> the sole treasure.
> In Jiva and Brahman, in man and God,
> In ghosts, and wraiths and spirits,
> and so forth.
> In Devas, beasts, birds, insects, and in worms,
> This Prema dwells in the heart of them all.
> (*In Search of God and Other Poems* 43)

In the above poem Swamiji says that nothing is greater than love, love may not be socially organized because it does not respects hurdles about it's revolution and growth. Even though un-conventional love carries it's own conditions of fulfillment which are trance rational moreover love does away with the distinction of forms and kinds because they are mere appearances and height the true essence. In one of his poems from *Song of Myself*, Walt Whitman said: "I think I could turn and live with animals/ they are so placid and self contain'd" (1). The *Jatika* stories of Buddha make Buddha proclaim that in his so many previous birth he has passed through many forms of life including animals and birds and each one of these birth he has learnt innumerable things:

> The mind, the Buddhi, chitta, Ahamkar,
> The Deva, Yaksha, man and demon, all—
> The quadruped, the bird, the worm,
> all insect life,
> The atom and its compound,
> all that is
> Animate and inanimate, all, all—
> The Internal and the External-dwell
> In that one common plane of
> Existence!
> (*In Search of God and Other Poems* 41)

In the poem above Vivekananda has made it clear that a truly religious person worships the creation of God as God himself he does not make any distinction between one form and another as all are portions of God. It is relevant to quote, Swami Ramtirtha, a contemporary of Vivekananda who use to say: "I don't believe in a God; I am part and parcel of him." Vivekananda refined Vedanta as polytheistically, monotheistic without disagreeing with Aadi Shankeracharya. Vivekananda does not make use of his concept of absolute monoism. For Swamiji Hinduism is not only the most ancient religion; it also found the basis of faith in other religions. This is so because Hinduism is not the name of the book; it is a way of life. Religious organizations do carry their own problems and they often do not entertain descends Hinduism, on the contrary is divided into multiple sects, philosophies which are often mutually contradictory to each other. This is precisely the strength of Hinduism. Consider the following line written by Rabindranath Tagore in his "Fireflies": "I am able to love my God/ because He gives me freedom to deny Him" (21). This is what found Hinduism. Now consider Vivekananda's interpretation of *Vedanta* as a belief in one-self, belief in a God who does not reside outside human bosom. Vivekananda said in one of his *Lectures from Colombo to Almora*:

> Faith, faith, faith in ourselves, Faith, faith in God—this is the secret of greatness. If you have faith in all the three hundred and thirty millions of your mythological gods, and in all the gods which foreigners have now and again introduced into your midst, and still have now faith in yourselves, there is no salvation for you. (101)

This clearly establishes Vivekananda's way of constituting faith. Faith is an endless texture; one who believes in one faith; cannot at the same time, disbelieve in other faiths.

The foregoing analysis of the poetry of Swami Vivekananda exhibits in ample measure the social function of poetry which is to eradicate evil and found the collective. Swamiji's poetry has many vital links with the poetry of *Tukaram, Kabir*, *Nanak* and the other poets of medieval devotional school of poetry. As remarked earlier Swamiji is a key renaissance figure and his kind is reconstitution of the principle subculture of religion upon which faith is founded. In very many ways Swamiji's poetry links itself with the west tradition of the romantic poetry as expounded by the German, the British and the American schools of romanticism. It is reformatory in character, intention and orientation cognitive intellectualism and live wire organism are the hallmarks of the poetry of the Vivekananda as that of romantic school of poetry. Swamiji thought that the seminal text of Indian tradition *Bhagavad Gita* is a romantic text not only because Krishna shows his cosmic form but also because it constitute faith in terms of *yogas—Karma yoga, Bhakti yoga, Raj yoga*, and *Jnana yoga*. The verse from the *Bhagavad Gita* with witch this paper began offers us with an optional variety which is face from doctrines, dogmas, rituals and regulatory bodies Vivekananda implies that religion is not the name of the book; it is the form of practice in the present this practice should manifest itself, with the service to the downtrodden, the unprivileged the poor and the destitute faith is never self-centered; faith is a form of continuous growth a distinctive kind of emergence within that envelopes the minutest as well as the biggest in its integrative fold. Vivekananda's methodology to arrive this place has been a critic of the local, the narrow and the lo-malice. This is something like separating grain from the chaff; one cannot separate the smell of the rose from the rose itself as for that matter Vivekananda is not asking for a change in the religion on prophecy. He is asking on the contrary, each one of us to understand our religion better than we do, I will end with a quotation from Swamiji "*Chicago Addresses*".

> I am a Hindu. I am sitting in my own little well and thinking that the whole world is my little well. The Christian sits in his little well and thinks the whole world is his well. The Mohammedan sits in his little well and thinks that is the whole world. I have to thank you of America for the great attempt you are making to break down the barriers of this little world of ours, and hope that, in the future the Lord will help you to accomplish your purpose. (24)

This clarifies that faith is inter-subjectively present in all of us. While religions can be understood as those of Hindu, Muslims and Christians faith is not dividable in such boundaries a child's laughter is not a Hindu or Muslim's laughter; it is simply child's laughter. It was in this spirit that Wordsworth says that "The child is father of the man" (1). Vivekananda offers this romantic canon of integration in his poetry and understands faith as a cosmic entity and not an individual. Originally God founded this world upon faith but man apparently lost it, Vivekananda as the true prophet of God, is trying to reconstitute the essentials of that faith upon once believes in oneself which shall lead to one believes in others.

WORKS CITED

Radhakrishnan, S. *The Bhagavadgita*. New Delhi: Harper Collins Publishers, 2010.

Tagore, Rabindranath. "Fireflies" in *Poems*. July 8, 2015 <http://www.allpoetry.com/>.

Vivekananda, Swami. *Chicago Addresses*. Kolkata: Advaita Ashrama, 2005, Reprint.

———. *In Search of God and Other Poems*. Kolkata: Advaita Ashrama, 2014, Reprint.

———. *Lectures from Colomobo to Almora*. Kolkata: Advaita Ashrama, 2005, Reprint.

Whitman, Walt. "I think I could Turn and Live with Animals" in *Song of Myself*. July 8, 2015 <http://www.allcreatures.org/>.

Wordsworth, William. "My Heart Leaps Up When I Behold" in *Online Books* at <http://www.bartleby.com/>. July 9, 2015.

A.K. Ramanujan's Poetry: A Shrine of Intellectual Insight

GAURI SHANKAR JHA

A.K. RAMANUJAN stands for genuine diaspora poetry of Indian writings in English that reflects, besides so many things, his intellectual insight coupled with other diasporic compulsions. The present paper investigates Ramanujan's specific instinct that enriches Indian English poetry enormously.

As we know, he spent his three decades of life at the United States and yet had persistent obsession with his Indian part, that is why, we prefer to term him as a diasporic priest. He grew up in a traditional middle class southern Brahmin family and possesses a bitter memory of 'a basketful of ritual cobras'. Though deeply immersed in the conventional design he does not accept everything blindly and yet as a diasporic entity he carves for his roots. While reading Girish Karnad, the outstanding playwright of Indian English Writing, the name of A.K. Ramanujan recurs most frequently, not as his companion but as his guide who helped him to comprehend the intellectual panorama of the Indian culture; Karnad is immensely indebted to Ramanujan's 'intellectual insight', he quotes his exchanges with him. A.B. Dharwadkar writes in the 'Introduction' of *Collected Plays* (Vol. II):

> At an intertextual level quite removed from the public life of the play, Tale-Danda, is also an extended tribute to A.K. Ramanujan, and the culmination of a long-standing intellectual relationship between the two leading post-independence authors from Karnataka. Karnad was drawn to his older contemporary from early adulthood because Ramanujan's brilliance as a poet, translator and scholar of Tamil and Kannada literature seemed to offer an exemplary model as well as an antithesis to his own interest as a playwright...he sometimes jocularly describes his entire creative career as an attempt to give antistic form to Ramanujan's intellectual insight.... Dedicated the 1989 English translation of 'Naga-Mandala' to Ramanujan in acknowledgement not only of the folktales he had passed along but the rich conversation

> between them that had circled endlessly around oral culture, folklore… through translation and commentary Ramanujan had accomplished the first major recuperation of this premodern socioreligious and literary movement…. In 'Tale-Danda' Karnad breathed a different kind of life into poetic texts and historical events by developing a dramatic structure that world 'explain' the relation of poetry and religious mysticism…. Following his mentor's example, he also avoided the sentimental simplifications…. (XIV-XV)

Such was the influence of Ramanujan over Karnad who is also taken to be a great intellectual of the day. As Shiv K. Kumar points out, "to the modern poet reality comes filtered through a juxtaposition of paradoxes" (3). We may cite the instance of 'Another View of Grace' where we may very easily diagnose the East-West encounter or say the clash of two distinctly polarized patterns of culture.

> Bred Brahmin among singers of shivering hymens I shudder to the bore at hungers that roam the streets beyond the constables beat. But there she stood upon that dusty road on a nightlit April mind and gave me a look. Commandments crumbled in my father's past. Her tumble hair suddenly known as silk in my angry hand, I shook a little and took her behind the laws of my land." (3)

Ramanujan feels the encounter of the two cultures within him "the Oriental which upholds restraint and the Western which permits unrestrained sexuality in the name of individual freedom" (3). He, as an inhibited Brahmin, finds himself helpless and his defence crumbling when he faces an American lady in the street, a foreign female with a lot of attraction. It is a sort of irony distinctly available in the post-Independence Indian English poetry, disturbing all facts of human experience: social, religious, moral or political. He is out to connect, that is, he believes in the wholeness of mankind, something like 'Vasudhaiv Kutumbkam', a sort of globalization, unification of the whole mankind; in his poem 'Connect' this voice can be heard,

> Connect! Connect—cries my disconnecting madness, resembling phrases. See the cycles. …Connect, beast with monks, slave economics and the golden bough.

He cannot betray his tradition, the ethics of Hinduism calls him ever; the title poem of the 'Second Sight' puts it clearly:

> You are a Hindoo, aren't you?/ You must have a Second Sight.

In the poem 'Waterfalls in a Bank', he trades back to his country: "As I transact with the past as with another country with its own customs, currency, stock exchange, always at a loss when I count my change."

Ramanujan has an astounding command over the vast treasure of Indian myths and folklore, which formed the theme of bulk of his poetry, a significant trait of postcolonial literature. It is this wide knowledge that bestows unambiguity to his world of creativity and could allure a titan like Girish Karnad, who quotes him to make the past relevant:

> Even in a large modern city like Madras, Bombay or Calcutta, even in Western-style nuclear families with their well planned 2.2 children, folklore…is only a suburb way, a cousin or a grandmother away. (315)

Karnad says, "It needs to be stressed here that these tales are not left-overs from the past" (315). G.K. Chestertan in his essay titled 'On Archeology' explains the petrifying effect of the past:

> We talk of the past as dead; but there is a very special and definite sense in which the past is always a living thing while the future is a dead thing. We know that the past has moved on living lines; but we can only conceive the future as moving on dead lines…the historic past is full of those free actions and frustrated prophecies…a man looking at the round arches of the old Roman and Norman architecture could not possibly have calculated from them that a hundred years afterwards, the delicate energy of the Gothic world be piercing the sky…if we want the wildest emotions of novelty and astonishment, we can only find them in mouldering stores and foding tapestries, in the museum of antiquities or the place of tombs. (11-15)

Lionet Trilling in his essay 'The Sense of the Past' says:

> The historical sense, that is, is to be understood as the critical sense, as the sense which life uses to test itself. …Mietzschis definition prescribes that culture be studied and judged as life's continuous evaluation of itself, the evaluation being understood as never finding full expression in the 'operating forces' of a culture, but as never finding full expression at all without reference to those gross institutional facts. (270-71)

It is very difficult to define human relationship and the factors which influence it: is it nature around us? is it culture that we inherit and continue? or is it something else which cannot be defined? This has been elaborated in the poems like 'Love Poem for a Wife and Her Trees' and 'Looking for the Centre'. It is but natural that physical reproduction occurs in the branches of 'family trees', 'with their roots in heaven/ and branches in the earth', it confirms that man is inextricably bound to the cosmos. The nexus with nature is paradoxical and imminent and he explains it in the poem 'One Move on a Deathless Theme': "Everyone in this street will become cold, like under stores or be scattered as ash in rivers and oceans." And then comes the term of time and culture forming the integral part of human life:

> Time moves in and out of me as stream of sound, a breeze, an electric current that seeks the ground.... Morning brown into evenings before I turn around in the day.

For Ramanujan, times is the cycle process of life, which keeps on rotating all the time and stream of humanity keeps on going unstopped. His poetry is replete with irony and in the words of Edward Said it is 'Worldly', coping with life as it is, rather an affirmation of it: "Yet days can be golden, apples beautiful if eyes can see only days and apples" ('If eyes can be').

It has been felt that in Indian English poetry a process of decolonization has taken place along with the political decolonization. Bruce King is of the view that it is a product of 'an independent nation and culture' (110) but we may easily rebut his assertion because Indian English poetry came into life before Independence though its 'British root' cannot be denied. He is also wrong in his observation that this school of poetry "seldom focus on local society and realities" (110). Ramanujan's poetry evolves out of Indian experience and sensibility, which includes "its memories of family, local places, images, beliefs and history," (115) often accused of being sceptical, ironical and unrealistic using conflict, argument and surprises. Even in the alien land, his hereditary Tamil Brahminism and south Indian culture does not betray him. Bruce King writes about his tools and techniques:

> The word play, puns, inner rhythms, rhetorical devices, ironies, distanced neutrality of tone, understatement, compression and elliptical progression the poems have similarities to his translations...highly aware of the conventions, techniques and structures of Indian verse and these have been used and transformed in his English poetry. (116)

His poetry is not immunised from the flow of modernity as he had extensive study of Yeats and Eliot; consequently, his poetry reveal 'complexity, instability and irony' of the moderns, most often based on old Indian poetic conventions and medieval poetry of sages. He traces the elements of modern science in classical Indian writings, though he practised Buddhist meditation. As Bruce King says:

> Everything is unstable, changing, transitory, predatory, striving to survive. He welcomed modernity but his sensibility was shaped by a view of life as repetitive cycles which have the appearance of change. (299)

He is also taken as 'the last major modernist, the poet of the perfect, concise, imagist lyric' (300). His poetry includes the influence of the modernists, and conventions of Tamil and Kannada poetics. In 'Introduction' to 'The Black Hen' Dharwadkar puts emphasis on the concern of Ramanujan with the body in relation to time and death. The black hen is an image suggestive of 'fertility and life' and its red eye is suggestive of anxiety and death: "The black hen stares with its round eye and you're afraid. It is in response to the prevalent romantic aesthetic." It comes sometimes as the black hen with the red round eye. Perhaps this is repercussions of *Upanishad* wisdom that he had acquired through extensive study of *Vedas* and *Upanishads* and we find it in the form of 'poetic inspiration, anxieties and death' which is also said to be the influence of the theory/vision of cause and effect, the cycle of life and death, etc., the larger views of life,

> I hear it running like an underground Ganges under my feet, over my head.... Always running from me.

In all the existence, life and death are intertwined and so for Ramanujan, every object has the potential to be studied. Later on he thought of propagating his ideas and revealed his philosophical vision with a deliberate inclusion of autobiographical ingredients, which also comprise his treatment of life as a sexual desire, longings of the flesh, particularly of the days after divorce and continual longing for her and his family. It has been alleged that Ramanujan acquaints us with 'similar ideas, phrases or images' (303) and also carries the conventions of medieval Tamil poetry. He had many close friends but his domestic life was a failure and it affect the philosophical and psychological theme of his poetry. Vilas Sarang is of the view that "Ramanujan's poetry springs out of deep inner compulsion, and is not merely the by-product of a well trained scholarly mind. True, there is a certain inhibited quality about Ramanujan's poetry...the inner turmoil...pretentions ambition...

strewn with references…inner and physical violence…derangement…. Psychosis…. Fear, anxiety and despair…darkness enters…" (24-25).

Keeping in view his diasporic identity his 'Relations' is more important because it reflects his maturity and serves as a bridge between his years at India and those at America. We have a taste of his bitterness in his reminiscence, "this little ounce of bitterness, this memory/ This load that weight a thousand tones, and yet/ is rich, bitter rich, because it is my life." Iyenger has called the essence of Ramanujan: 'Oh God, oh God, oh misgotten One!' 'You fool, there is no promised land….' And then the mysterious man that he finds everywhere: "I touched him. He was not there. He fled, laughing, weeping. Yet he was next to me. Where did he live?" An hotel room. I asked him who he was. He said mockingly: "Can't you guess?/ I am loneliness." It is all in the seventeen pieces of Leslie de Noronha's 'Poem' whose last poem is most remarkable:

> That I must harbour the silent chalice of self-Knowledge, Bitterly, profoundly
>
> My hatred a glorious requiem/
> A hymn, a symphony….

M.K. Naik quotes him as "the most outstanding poet of the sixties… another exile" (199). To understand the constitution of the poetic sensibility and mental make-up of Ramanujan it is very important to take care of his own confession as quoted by R. Parthasarthy in his book *Ten Twentieth Century Indian Poets* (Delhi: 1976: 95-96). M.K. Naik quotes further:

> English and my disciplines (linguistics, anthropology) give me my 'outer' forms—linguistic, metrical, logical and other such ways of shaping experience, and my thirty years in India, my frequent visits and field trips, my personal and professional preoccupations with Kannada, Tamil, the classes and folklore give me my substance, my 'inner' forms, images, symbols. (200)

Obviously, his poetry is burdened with his 'racial burden', 'Hindu heritage', 'Ancestral crocodiles and tortoise' and, no doubt, domestic upheavals. Yet he is aware of the worth and imperfections, sustenance and limitations of these ethos. He holds in esteem its values in the poem 'Christmas' which celebrate the 'Vision of Unity of All Life': "leaf from parrot or branch from root, nor…that tree from you or me." He admits his mission as his weakness or limitation: "I must seek and will find/ My particular hell in my Hindu mind."

After all, he is a modern Hindu and so he can trace the gap/rift between the traditional and modern Hindu entity explicit in his poems; his utterances are noteworthy:

'The Hindoo: he reads his Gita and is calm at all events'

'The Hindoo: he doesn't Hunt a fly or spider either.'

M.K. Naik says: "His articulation of the Hindu ethos has so far produced (with a few notable exceptions) poetry of the periphery and not the centre of the Hindu experience" (202).

His relation with Hinduism is precariously designed and so M.K. Naik says:

> A later poem like 'Prayers to Lord Murugan' even reveals a curious uncertainly in his reaction to Hinduism. Perhaps Ramanujan has yet to come fully to terms with his heritage and is still feeling his way. Meanwhile, he has effectively demonstrated to his contemporaries the supreme importance of having roots and has also shown glimpses of the vitality the work of a poet acquires when he succeeds even partially in his attempt. (202)

K.V. Surendran in his book *Indian English Poetry: New Perspective* writes:

> Parthasarthy has observed that the quality of experience he would like to express in English and the quality of the Indian he uses are the twin problems for an Indian writing in English. A.K. Ramanujan who can certainly be referred to as the poet of the Indian sensibility in one is able to easily and effortlessly survive both these problems. He successfully turned the ordinary into the exotic and the exotic into the ordinary. His poems are noted for their variety and the skilled use of the language. (710)

It is very important to note that the post-Independence poetry suffers from a peculiar kind of vacuum after the departure of the British. As O.P. Bhatnagar point out: "The end of slavery is the beginning of the freedom to be free. The sudden departure of the British from India made Indian confront a variety of anomalies, conflicts, contradictions and paradoxes welling up their subconscious, necessitating redefinition of their roles and commitments in the changed context of the times...felt more keenly in Indian poetry in English. The most important dilemma the poet felt was one of alienation in their own land and therefore the paradox of belonging" (199). Regarding A.K. Ramanujan he says:

> A.K. Ramanujan turned to history, tradition, myth, literature and family to contain the alienation of the self forced by his stay away from his roots, abroad. In him the modern mind comes face to face with tension of having a 'home' back home…a man settled abroad…. In him the problems of life and poetry converge polishing images, irony and reflective skill…his Indian psyche and identity alive in a foreign land and also accept the plurality of identity. (210-11)

His diasporic identity provides an additional quality in asserting and analysing a situation or an individual or a mythology. He strides back objectively and approaches his personal concern most often to generalize and universalize it in a unique way, that is, the approach is Indian but the modality is Western, taken it other round while the selling is Western, the mode of observation is Indian; thus the first poem of 'The Striders' (1966) has the image of New England water insect, the most effective poetic technique to convey his feeling:

> And search for certain this-stemmed, bubble-eyed water bugs. See them perch/ On dry capillary legs. Weightless on the ripple skin of a stream. No, not only prophets walk on water. This bug sits on a landslide of lights and drowns eye-deep into its tiny strip of sky. (*The Striders*)

His two faculties of reasoning and sentiment from a balance and suggest a relationship which dictates his ideology and mission:

> ….Water is all eyes. The earth has bone for muscle. And the air is a flock of invincible pigeons. But anxiety can find no metaphor to end it. (Anxiety)

His endeavour is to define his own self, his own personality, his own being, and in order to do so he is a bit sceptic and philosophical:

> I resemble everyone but myself, and sometimes see in shop windows despite the well-known laws of optics the portrait of stranger date unknown. Often signed in a corner by my father. (Self Portrait)

The inherited Hinduism and the *sanskar* tortures him and his poetic self is, most of the time, at war with the fanatic sensibilities with a pinch of ironic stance, and finally, there is the triumph of his poetic sensibility, and the impossible ideals of Hinduism is defected; consequently, the incongruities and contradictions surface, for instance, the philosophy of detachment in Hinduism is both a riddle and the target of ridicule:

> At the bottom of all this bottomless enterprise to keep simple hearts gain beat the only risk is heartlessness." (The Hindu: the only Risk)

He reasons his memories as a detached critic and his emotional self lies flat against such irony trains of his poetic self:

> Memory in a crowd of memories, seems to have no place at all for unforgettable things. ("On Memory". *The Striders*)

Such memories are inadequate tools to investigate the past, that is, the convention, the tradition, the *sanskar* and the roots, which on the other hand, help him to discover and rediscover his own self; though this technique of self-discovery he discovers the vicinity, the universe and the whole mankind; so, it is a journey from selfhood to the rest of the universe, a sort of globalisation of the self. This expression of self also acquaints him with the strength and weakness of his own self and the entire humanity on the whole; it is his diasporic self which rebels against his conventional background:

> I am lined on branches bare as roots without that latest hatch of births-bewildered parrots. (Christmas)

Here, he scrutinizes his own self and the situation is best brought out by a leafless free being watered by an Indian in the USA. His discovery is a continual process of search for the self to establish "a pattern of permanence in the flux/flow of personal experience turning poetry of reverie into the poetry of immediacy or authenticity, a kind of juxtaposition of the poetic experience of reality and the search for the self" (213). And so he discovers:

> I cannot unlearn conventions of despair. They have their pride I must seek and will find my particular hell only in my Hindu mind. ("Conventions of Despair". *The Striders*)

And his nostalgic earnestness resonates further trade back, roll to past to locate the epicentre, the pivotal point:

> Something opened in the past and I heard something shut in the future, quietly like the heavy door of my mother's black pillared nineteenth century silent house, given on her marriage day to my father, for a dowry. ("Still Another for Mother". *The Striders*)

In the poem 'Small Scale Reflection on a Great House', he is haunted by ideas instead of nostalgia:

> And ideas behave like rumours one casually mentioned somewhere they came back to the door as prodigies born to prodigal father with eyes that vaguely look our own.

Besides, the Hinduism and its rituals, personal life and family, India and its way of life, Ramanujan lapses into the spiritual world, the supreme power of Almighty and His abode, which we may call a positive force or a divine compulsion or a sort of enlightenment towards creative urge of life and towards the value under preservation and perceptions of their place in a man, family, society and the world at large and so he says in 'A Poem on Particulars':

> I have heard it said among the planters you can sometimes count every orange on a tree but never all the trees in a single orange.

In the poem 'The Watchers', Ramanujan is obsessed with the truth as essence of life and the inability of the poet to convey us,

> Lighter than light, blowing like air through keyholes, they watch without questions the watchers; they watch even the questions as I live over and over with concealed stamps on verandas.

Ramanujan's poetic self evolves to maturity in the poem 'Chicago Zen', in the process of self-exploration and discovery of one's own entity:

> Now you know what you always know; the country cannot be reached by jet. Nor by boat or jungle river…. But only by answering ordinary black telephones, questions walls and small children ask and answering all call of nature.

This is a sort of resolution that the poet makes in order to console himself and acquaint himself with the ongoing of the world, the flux of morality, humanity, values and the stance of the world.

Diverse cultural influences operate simultaneously in the making of a postcolonial and postmodern poet and his diasporic entity which we may call as an instance of polished, sophisticated and profound multiculturalism—Ramanujan is such a poet and his poetry accommodates linguistic, literary and cultural features and farms of Tamil, Kannada and English literature. N. Sharada Iyenger in his paper 'The Portrait of an Artist' quotes Rama Jha's interview with Ramanujan which is relevant to quote here:

> One cannot live in the past, neither can you entirely live in the present, because we are not like that. The past never passes. Either the individual past a historical past or cultural past. It is with us, it is what gives us the richness…of understanding. And the richness of expression…creativity comes out of a sustained attention to one's own experience, one's own locality and one's own landscape you

> know. And the circumstances which one can feel and experience deeply without any scheme, without bearing this, that and other... whatever world it may be. It may be a personal world, it may be a social world, but a world which is fully embodied in poetry. We need enough of that, same part of our experience—to explore it as best as we can. (124)

As an expatriate, Ramanujan lives in two worlds at once, one within and the one without, one Indian and the other Western. Vasant A. Shahana and M. Sivarama Krishna in their paper titled "Indian Poetry in English: A Critical Assessment" says:

> Ramanujan and his contemporaries Ezekiel and Kamala Das exhibit in their poetry three concentric circles of self in relation to society, self in relation to history with family as the core unit and self in relation to itself, its own propelled emotions and feelings. (127)

Taken as a whole Ramanujan's poetry is an outstanding amalgamation of his experience of the bitter truth of life, his deep attachment with his family members, his inherited Hindu sentiments, heave of his knowledge of mythology both Tamil and Kannad and the fascination of the West—all treated with intellectual insight of diasporic torn self.

WORKS CITED

Bhatnagar, O.P. *Poetry as Discovery* in *Studies in Indian Poetry in English*. Eds. A.N. Prasad & U.S. Rukhaiyar. New Delhi: Sarup & Sons Pub., 2002.

Chesterton, G.K. *On Archeology,* in *English Prose & Poetry Selection*. Gauhati University, University Publication Department, 1995.

Dharwadkar, A.B. *Collected Plays* (Vol. II). New Delhi: O.U.P., 2008.

Iyenger, K.R.S. *Indian Writing in English.* New Delhi: Sterling Pub., 2003.

Iyer, N.S. *The Portrait of an Artist,* in *Studies in Indian Poetry in English*. Eds. A.N. Prasad & U.S. Rukhaiyar. New Delhi: Sarup & Sons Pub., 2002.

King, Bruce. *Modern Indian Poetry in English*. New Delhi: O.U.P., 2001.

Kumar, Shiv K. *Contemporary Indian Literature in English*. Shimla: I.I.A.S., 1992.

Nagrajan, S. *Contemporary Indian Poetry in English*. Ed. Saleem Peeradina. Madras: Macmillan, 1977.

Naik, A. *History of Indian English Literature*. New Delhi: Sahitya Akademi, 1999.

Naik, M.K. *Indian English Poetry: From the beginning upto 2000*. Delhi: Pencraft, 2006.

Sarang, Vilas. *Indian English Poetry since 1950: An Anthology*. Mumbai: Orient Longman, 1989.

Surendran, K.V. *Indian English Poetry*. New Delhi: Sarup & Sons Pub., 2002.

Trilling, Lionel. *The Sense of the Past*, in *Literary Criticism: A Reading.* Ed. B.B. Das & J.M. Mohanty, New Delhi: O.U.P., 2005.

Vasant A. Shahana and M. Sivarama Krishna. Eds. *Indian Poetry in English: A Critical Assessment*. Delhi: Macmillan, 1980.

Statement about Ownership and other Particulars of
The Atlantic Critical Review

FORM IV (See Rule 8)

Place of Publication	:	New Delhi
Periodicity of the Publication	:	Quarterly
Printer's Name	:	Manish Kumar
Nationality	:	Indian
Address	:	B-2, Vishal Enclave, New Delhi 110027
Publisher's Name	:	Manish Kumar
Nationality	:	Indian
Address	:	B-2, Vishal Enclave, New Delhi 110027
Editor's Name	:	Sunita Sinha
Nationality	:	Indian
Address	:	402, Rameshwaram Apartment, Miss Mandal Compound, East Boring Canal Road, Patna, Bihar
Names and addresses of individuals who own the newspaper and partners or shareholders holding more than one per cent of the total capital	:	K.R. Gupta B-2, Vishal Enclave New Delhi-110027

I, Manish Kumar, hereby declare that the particulars given above are true to the best of my knowledge and belief.

Sd/-

Date : 1st July, 2015

MANISH KUMAR
Publisher

Voices from the Margin in the Plays of Vijay Tendulkar

AMAR NATH PRASAD

VIJAY TENDULKAR, a journalist by profession, is a problem play writer. In almost all his plays he raises some social maladies, particularly associated with the voices of the margin. He is fond of describing vultures of society, exploiters, sadists, predators and some atavistic behavior. He wants to root out the evils of the world by examining critically and exposing dauntlessly and provocatively. But his dramatic portrayal of social ills and maladies is not simply historical, dry and monotonous, rather it is suffused with various dramatic and poetic devices. He has an equal command of both feeling and form, matter and manner. His images, symbols and metaphors are very suggestive; so far as the dramatic pageant and presentation is concerned, Tendulkar seems to be a master craftsman with an unslipping grip on the various techniques of dramatic art. He has given the post-independence Marathi drama a new idiom and a new vision and thus put the Marathi drama on the national and international map.

Vijay Tendulkar has to his credit 30 full length plays, 23 one act plays and a number of screen plays for Marathi movies. Vijay Tendulkar's famous play "Silence The Court is in Session" is a play which deals with the voice of the marginalised woman. It shows the plight and predicament of a woman whose bodily wealth is plundered by a gang of selfish men. It is the story of one Miss Leela Benare, a dutiful and punctual school teacher, who becomes the victim of the carnal lust of some men who seldom take care of her modesty and her ardent wish to live a peaceful and domestic life of the husband and wife. In technique, the play is artistically structured and contains almost all the features of a modern problem play. Some of the images and symbols of this book are highly suggestive. They speak volumes of things in a nutshell.

The play opens with the ridicules and banter of the characters of the actual play. The real play is scheduled to be staged in the night. The characters have a lot of time; so they want to rehearse the actual drama.

A mock trial is staged in which a woman is put to trial for her offence of infanticide. Miss. Benare has to perform the role of this woman. All the members of the troupe except Prof. Damle are present. At first the trial begins with the humorous posture, ridicules, laughter and caricature; but in the third act, the play becomes more grave and critical. Miss Benare reveals her secret. She exposes the hypocrisy of some men who uprooted her plant of life. She tells how she was deflowered by her own maternal uncle at the age of fourteen:

> Why, I was hardly fourteen! I didn't even know what sin was—I swear by my mother, I didn't! I insisted on marriage. So I could live my beautiful lovely dreams openly. Like anyone else! But all of them—my mother too—were against it. And my brave man turned tail and ran.[1]

After this traumatic experience she felt like a fish out of water. She wanted to commit suicide, but she didn't. She searched for an identity of her own in an entirely adverse society where men have little love for women; where men are hungry for the bodily pleasures of women. Inspite of her previous error once again she falls in love with Prof. Damle. But now this love is not unconscious and ignorant as it was with her maternal uncle. But this new life again deserts her. She narrates:

> Again, I fell in love. As a grown woman. I throw all my heart into it. I thought, this will be different. This love is intelligent. It is love for an unusual intellect. It is not love at all—its worship! But it was the same mistake. I offered up my body on the altar of my worship. And my intellectual god took the offering and went his way. He didn't want my mind or my devotion—didn't care about them! He was not a god. He was a man, for everything was the body, for the body! That is all![2]

Thus, this is a tragic story of the plight of a woman who is facing an identity crisis in a male-dominated patriarchal framework where even women are not helpful to women rather they needle and pinpoint in the hour of critical juncture of the protagonist. This piteous predicament reminds us of Arundhati Roy's Booker prize winning book *The God of Small Things* in which Ammu, the protagonist has to move from pillar to post and has to face various trials and tribulations, cares and anxieties without any rhyme or reason. It also reminds us of the various women characters of Shashi Deshpande who have to bear the brunt of silent suffering engendered by the cruel and callous society—mostly dominated by men.

Well, Miss Leela Benare commits her incestuous relation in an ignorant stage charmed under a juvenile frenzy. But when she comes of age she commits a conscious and adult bodily relation with Prof. Damle whom she worshipped as a god. But this god took the offering of her body and turned his back to her. This humiliation was unbearable to a forsaken woman who is in the constant search of an identity of a married woman. Inspite of all these unbearable physical and mental tortures and humiliations, she doesn't surrender! Rather she wants to lead a life—a new life. But some men in society are jealous to her. They always taunt and jeer at her. In the very beginning of the play, we see their taunts and jeers. Even Mrs. Kashikar is not an exception. Being a woman she doesnot even help the helpless Benare. But Mrs. Benare is the perfect character who leads her life as a whole forgetting all her previous traumatic experiences:

> Benare: Forget about the sage Tukaram. I say it—I Leela Benare, a living woman, I say it from my own experience. Life is not meant for anyone else. It is your own life. It must be it's very, very important thing, every moment, every bit of it is precious.[3]

The story takes a serious turn in the last act in which we see how a helpless bird (Miss Leela Benare) is surrounded by the hungry vultures (the other characters). We also notice the manifestation of physical violence when Rokde is asked to conduct the accused, Miss Benare, to the witness box. Mrs. Kashikar drags her very roughly and rudely to the witness box. Benare, on the other hand, is dumb-founded. She is unable to speak anything. This shows how a progressive woman like Benare has to face several hazards and obstacles silently. Despite several unbecoming reprimands, she doesnot answer any of their rubbish question—"why is she unmarried".

It is interesting to note here that Mrs. Kashikar represents here a traditional housewife who has nothing to do with the progressive and modern attitude of a young girl in the modern scientific world. She thinks that her whole life is the family in which she is brought up and for which happiness she has to lead a future life. But, on the other hand, Miss Benare represents a progressive, educative and changing life. She wants to come out from the clutches of patriarchal domination. She wants to lead a life of her own—a life which is free from the conservative norms of society. She is like Shelley's 'winged seeds', that want to bloom and sprout; but they are covered with the 'dead leaves' or the 'sapelss foliage'. To change the metaphor, she is an 'unextinguished hearth'[4] where the sparks of her attitude and wish to live a new married life has been subdued by the ashes of the rotten codes and norms of the society. And in this respect what hinders most in the smooth way of a progressive woman is no one but a woman in particular and other societal codes in general.

Well, Miss Benare is a silent sufferer. She has a great patience to suffer. She is the embodiment of innocence and compassion. Though she is victimized at every step, she has done harm to none. If she did harm to anybody, it is her own self. Prof. Damle made an illicit relation with her to slake his sexual thirst. But just after quenching his carnal desires and making her pregnant, he deserts her. But in spite of all these things, she has no illwill against him. Mr. Ponkshe says:

> No, first she said, "Please don't call him a scoundrel. He may be a good man. He may be very great and wise. She may have fallen short. She may not have been able to convince him how deeply she feels for him. The woman is not the crucial factor. It is the boby that comes first."[5]

The plight and plunder of a helpless woman has been best expressed in the apt placements of irony in the play. In this play, Miss Benare has been given the role of a prisoner. But truly speaking it is not Miss Benare who is the prisoner; she is free from the fear of society. She has her own will. But the other characters are really prisoners as they are not free from their pretensions, hypocrisy, mental disorders, inferiority complexes, so on and so forth. The term 'silence' is itself ironic. At first it shows the silence of the court, which must be maintained at any cost as the decorum of the courts demands. But we see that the culprits are very vocal and impulsive while the protagonist is silent at first. But when the false speeches and untruthful impositions of the lawyers and other actors cross the limit of decorum and decency of a court and the private life of a woman, the rebellious woman in Benare explodes and does a great havoc making all the listeners dumb-founded. It is the last speech of her which may be called the heart of the play. This speech has been very consciously and thoughfully constructed by the skilled playwrite. It has been woven into the fabric of art and literature, irony and pathos. She says:

> But I was ignorant, instead I threw myself off a parapet of our house —to embrace death. But I didn't die. My boy didn't die. I felt as if feeling were dead—but they hadn't died either then.[6]

Thus, the brief survey of the play shows that the play is beset with various examples of plights and plunders deliberately engendered by the terrible monsters of the society. Here the plight of woman is not simply working on the physical ground but it is deeprooted to the psychological torturing to a forsaken woman who is constantly searching for an anchor to cover the misdeeds and injustice of the male folk. It is the realistic exposure of the hypocrisy, pretensions and male chauvinism of some self-centered people who treat woman like flowers in their pot or to change a bitter metaphor, they quench their bodily thirst like a lascivious animal and than desert her to her own fate. This animality or even worse than animality in this play seems to fling an unpalatable irony on our rich cultural heritages where women are worshipped as a deity and imagined as a great source of fertility and heavenly values of life.

Vijay Tendulkar's other well-known play *Ghashiram Kotwal* also portrays the voices of the marginalized. We see that how a woman like Lalita Gouri is helpless in this play. Her father even goes to the extent of making her a rubber stamp of power and glory. On the other hand, we also see that how a sexually hungry person like Nana Phadnavis is quite adamant and rigid to slake his sexual thirst with his beautiful young girl. And the climax is that she is left for dying in her pregnancy. She has to meet a very shameful death.

The Sutradhar presents a very realistic picture of the women of the corrupted Brahmins of Poona. He says:

> The Brahmans have lost themselves in the Kirtan: the Brahman women are sentenced to solitary confinement.[7]

This play also contains the theme of class discrimination. Here in this play a clash between the rich and the poor, the low and the high is quite obvious, Ghashiram and the helpless woman represent the lower section of society while Nana Phadnavis and the Brahmins of Poona, the higher section of society. The people of the higher seetion of society don't want to see the rise of a poor and low character like Ghashiram. When Ghashiram becomes the Kotwal of the town, it becomes indigestible to them. They want to uproot him by hook or crook. On the other hand, Ghashiram kotwal is also suffering from the politics of caste. He, like Kalo of the novel "He who Rides a Tiger" by Bhabani Bhattacharya, wants to take revenge of his humiliation and undeserved persecution. He gives undeserved punishment to the Brahmins. He even goes to the extent of punishing the innocent and the poor without any rhyme or reason, only to satisfy his humiliation. In other words, there is so much chaos and upheaval, that is a state without proper administration. The administration is not centered to only one hand but it is centrifugal. Sutradhar, in an ironic tone rightly says: Gauri orders, Nana does, Ghashiram reigns.[8]

Vulgarity and sexuality also play an important role in the texture of the play. Through this play, Tendulkar has exposed the decadence of the age—its sexuality and vulgarity, hypocrisy and moral and spiritual breakdown. As the play opens, the Sutradhar inquires the Brahmins who are going to Bavannakhani, a place where there is nothing but immorality and vulgarity in the name of group dancing and religious chanting. The Sutradhar says:

> Nana goes. The Brahmins stay. No restrictions now. No reverence now. No modesty now. No protocol now. None at all.[9]

The immorality can also be seen in the speech and behavior of Nana Phadnavis. In a 'lavani' dance, Nana comes in contact with a beautiful girl. He jeers at her. He looks unblinkingly to this pretty girl. He walks towards the girl like a cat. All go but the girl is alone in the room. Nana gestures to the servant to close the door. In a very vulgar tone he proposes to the girl:

> Oh, don't be shy. This is our house. This is a private hall. No one will see. No one in Poona today has the audacity to watch the great Nana Phadnavis.[10]

Thus the play is an amalgam of various themes. It is the greatness of Vijay Tendulkar that he has presented the drab reality of the contemporary society not through dry and monotonous language but through wit and humour, technique and craftsmanship. In the hands of Tendulkar the theme of savagery and vulgarity has got a new colour.

Among the plays of Vijay Tendulkar, 'Sukhram Binder' is the most controversial one. It is also based on the theme of "Women victimization". The central character of this play is Sukhram who is a lower middle class book binder who has an insatiable appetite for female sex. In order to satisfy his sexual hunger, he gives shelter to helpless women on his own terms. He keeps one woman at a time and he accepts that he is a habitual womanizer. He is also a drunkard and in a fit of intoxication of wine, he sometimes makes an anatomy of the hypocrisy and deception of society. At first Laxmi comes in contact with him. But after sometime Sukhram is fed up with her as she was very religious, docile and devoted to worship. So, he sends her away to her nepnew. Soon he comes in contact with another woman Champa who is opposite to Laxmi and makes him more sensuous, lewd and licentious. But there is some milk of human kindness in the character of Champa. She asks Sukhram to bring back Laxmi to his house. After being driven away by her nephew, Laxmi once again returns to the house of Sukhram. But there too, her survival is threatened by the presence of Champa. As a result, Laxmi, though she was not willy and vicious, conspires a plan to drive away Champa from the house. She reveals Champa's illicit relation with Dawood to Sukhram. Sukhram becomes very wild with anger and throttles Champa with his hands and cries out "Murder! Murder". At this critical juncture, Laxmi comes and controls the situation and helps the defeated Sukhram. So, like the play *Gidhade*, here we get lust, but not the lust of money but the lust of body; Champa takes Sukhram to the deeper and deeper hell of lust, as a result, she gets punishment at the end of the play.

Tendulkar's *Kamala* is a play which can be placed under "The Theatre of Cruelty". The theatre of cruelty may be seen in abundance in the trinity of the Greek tragic writers—Aeschylus, Sophocles and Euripedes. Anotonine Artoud, the French writer resuscitated the theme of cruelty. He opines that there is a task for crime, sexuality and savageness in the psyche of human being. He also thinks that a play must 'first disturb our happiness and peace of mind and then release our suppressed sub-conscious. The philosophy of cruelty exercised a great influence on the plays of Vijay Tendulkar, particularly on his *Kamala*.

The central character of this drama is Jaisingh Jadhav a selfish man who purchased woman from the flesh market and treats them as an object.

Kamala, an adivasi woman is bought by Jaisingh Jadhav at the flesh market of Lohardaga for two hundred and fifty rupees. As the story goes on we see how Kamala has to live a life of slavery. Jaisingh Jadhav doesn't allow her to do anything according to her will. He is unkind and inconsiderate to all the women including his wife, Sarita who rightly sums up his character;

> ...a man who is in the year 1982 still keeps a slave, right here in Delhi, Jaisingh Jadhav. I am going to say: this man is a great advocate of freedom. And he brings home a slave and exploits her.

> One can use and throw away. He gets people to call him a sworn enemy of tyranny. But he tyranises his own slave as much as he likes and does not think of it—nothing at all.[11]

Thus, in this play, Jaisingh Jadhav represents the male domination over woman and a bourgeois mentality in society which seldom cares for the weak and the downtrodden. He deserts Kamala when his purpose is served. Talking to Sunil Shambag. Vijay Tendulkar observes:

> …Kamala after a time becomes a symbol. The wife of the Journalist becomes 'Kamala' and ultimately even he (Journalist) becomes 'Kamala'.[12]

To sum up, Tendulkar's plays make the anatomy of society in a very realistic way with the help of some hard and concrete images and symbols. In almost all the plays, we find a contrast between the good and the evil, the rough and the sublime, the ruler and the ruled. The beauty of his plays lies in his art of well-knit plot and characterization, his exposure of the sham and hypocrisy of the evil world, his apt use of irony and humour and, above all, the portrayal of the past in the context of the present. His constant efforts for raising the voice of the voiceless will ever by remembered not only by the connoisseurs of art, literature and drama but also by the social scientists and workers who want to study the subalterns and the voiceless in totality.

REFERENCES

1. Tendulkar, Vijay, *Silence! The Court is in Session*, Oxford University Press, Delhi, 1992: 74.
2. *Ibid.*, 74-75.
3. *Ibid.*, 8.
4. The phrases under inverted commas have been taken from the poem "Ode to the West Wind" by P.B. Shelley.
5. Tendulkar, Vijay, *op. cit.*, 63.
6. *Ibid.*, 74.
7. Tendulkar, Vijay, '*Ghashiram Kotwal*', Seagull Book, Kolkata, 2002.
8. *Ibid.*, 26.
9. *Ibid.*, 21.
10. *Ibid.*, 28.
11. *Kamala* translated by Priya Adarkar, *Five Plays*, Oxford University Press, 1974: 46.
12. Tendulkar, Vijay, 'I am against sensational Journalism', *The Sunday Observer*, October, 1982.

Lawrence: Exploration and Exposition of The Self

N. SHARADA IYER

D.H. LAWRENCE in his letter, essays, poetry and fiction holds that literature depends on philosophy, needed philosophical contents. While actually engaged in working at his aesthetic vision a writer might not at all be conscious of the philosophical nature of his theme. He further speaks of the absolute need of formulating some "definite conclusions out of a completed work of fiction if one is to come to terms with the experience offered. Lawrence like Thomas Hardy used the novel to present his own view of life. Both were concerned with the basic problems of human existence—man's relationship with his fellowmen, with the universe beyond himself. He combined a violent hatred of modern mechanical civilization. He came to feel the deadness of modern industrial civilization, with the assertion of personalities, the corruption of the will and the dominance of the sterile intellect over the inward passion of man, which Lawrence saw as the inevitable accompaniment of modern life.

> "The growing materialism and selfishness, the increasing ugliness, sordidness
> And meanness shocked him and he reacted with characteristic violence"

The war intensified his disgust of the huge obscene machine to the effect of which his childhood and youth had been prematurely exposed to. It made him rebel against all the accepted values of modern Western civilization. He challenged the disintegration not only of those who were actually caught in the blind mechanism of industries but also of all those who reflected materialism, he considered them to be one of hard possessiveness, devoid of emotions to become sterile intellectuals.

He could not have created this antagonism with such magnetic force and insight if he had not experienced to an abnormal degree by himself. Endowed with a physical and mental sensibility he personified as only a genius obsessed beyond the possibility of human tolerance could the suffering of a self-conscious mind, exasperated by the soulless clamor of machinery, stifled by the fumes of all its wasteful products, and seeking frantically to recover peace, harmony and health by a return to the primitive. It was this which took him to Italy, Sicily, Mexico, Sardinia and India. He sought the unity of instinctive life by self-conscious thoughts among the beasts, birds, reptile, ferns, flowers, fruits and even mosquitoes.

With a love for the primitive and natural, with a passionate belief in the importance in the development of each individual "the slow building up of the integral person through the years". Scorning the mere intellectual faculty—which depriving life of its thrill, vitality and gaiety—he placed his thrust in the experiences of the senses which for him seemed to gain in value as they became forceful. Man's primitive instinct and impulses which spring from his unconscious mind are the safest guides for life "All I want is to answer to my blood, direct without the fribbling intervention of the mind, or moral or what not."

Lawrence's Hell is the mechanized world of factories, jazz and cinema, a world where everything is experienced in the head. His Heaven is the beauty of nature unspoiled "Like a neo-romantic he yearns for contact with the earth and is filled with nostalgia for the bright sensuous life that town life is steadily destroying" writes Baker. His philosophy represents the revolt of the man of nature...the possessive greed of the modern man which inflicts such misery on instincts and impulses. In *Sons and Lovers* Lawrence presents the ugliness of the industrial life and the Wilbury factory. Walter Morel Gertrudes' marriage fail. He is driven often to the pub and is finally destroyed.

At times he talked as a wild anarchist, asserting that everything must be pulled down or blown up, so that a new start could be made. But he had no patience with political or social panacea, he is concerned always with human relationship. With the possibility of fulfillment and exposing all the dead formulation about romantic love, marriage, friendship good life which can cause so much deadness, frustration, and distortion in the life of an individual. He found that education was all arranged in terms of standard rather than that of person. All the branches of education—literature, history, theology, religion—all these went to prove that everything was the same. He knew himself to be an extraordinary young man wanting to achieve high ideals, but he found that this was a rule not an exception.

Lawrence felt he was being pushed into something, not only the way of life but to impose something on him of which they themselves were hurt greatly feared from. He might have got to know the curious world, might have made it a part of him, but he could not manage it, he felt he was being engulfed by it. He was not going to wander between two worlds one dead and the other powerless to be born. Life which he began to think of being full of dead mode of living, what he did was to turn away from the dead mode of living with hatred, convinced that everything connected with it was evil, and everything opposite to it was good.

Lawrence wrote in *Lady Chatterley's Lover* "Ours is an essentially tragic age, and he traces the root of this tragedy to the over intellectualism of life due to advancement of science. Science with its emphasis on reason destroys the intuitional and intuitive life of man. There is every likelihood of man achieving happiness if he relies more on impulse than on reason. Reason is likely to distort his vision of reality but his impulses if un-spoiled by external influences will never mislead him. In this respect he is one with the Romantics, with Rousseau, with Wordsworth who wanted to go back to the elemental simplicities of life, with John Keats who yearned for a life of pure sensation. Like a true Romantic he yearns for contact with the earth, fillid with nostalgia for the bright sensory life that modern civilization is steadily destroying" comments Diana Nell.

Lawrence rejects reason as something fatal to life, something that deprived life of its joys and saps its vitality. In a letter to his friend Ernest Collins expresses his faith in the religion of blood:

> My own religion is a belief in the blood, the 'flesh as being wiser than the intellect. We can go wrong in our mind. But what our blood feels and believes and says is always true. The reason is only a bit and a bridle. What do I care about knowledge. All I want is to answer to my blood, direct without the fribbling intervention of the mind, moral or what not I conceive of man's body as a flame, like a candle ever upright and yet flowing: and the intellect as just the light that is shed on the things around.

In *Sons and Lovers, The White Peacock, The Rainbow, Lady Chatterley's Lover* he focused on the subject of sex and sought to raise it to the level of spiritual. He was misunderstood, books banned, branded as a writer of the obscene, vulgar and pornographic themes, but that did not deter him from writing on his chosen path. In *Sons and Lovers* he stated:

> I want men and women to be able to think sex fully, completely honestly and clearly....
>
> Men cannot deny the need of the body. One has to give to Christ what he needs and to Caesar what is a kings.

He was a prophet of the primitive instinct and passion. Lawrence's work is saturated in sex, even when it is devoid of sexual incidents. So powerful is the obsession that the author seldom finds it necessary to state at the most unexpected moment that this or that emotion was 'sexless'. The effect of this is to focus attention on sex even when sex is being expressively denied.

Lawrence had the courage and conviction to write boldly of matters which he considered to be of great importance. His approach may be non-moral and non-intellectual, but it is of value so far as it throws light on the possible human situation in which man finds himself in today. Sex element is part of his versatile genius. He deals with it not because he does but because he thought he must deal with it.

Lawrence feels that the modern man is unhappy because he has been denied full and complete life, and has lost all sense of community, and because he is nothing inside. Lawrence had nothing but intense anger for science and technology and man's materialistic attitude. Its sinister influence has fragmented man, thus making him incapable of making a full and total response to the mystery of life.

"The scientific civilization is based on an abstract, incoherent orientation towards life—and this is the way of death alone, Lawrence sees nothing but total stagnation in such an approach. He therefore pleads for a physical, organic and non-intellectual orientation to life."

Lawrence's main concern is to realize a whole and organic life, and this is possible only when man realizes his three relationships—relationship with the living universe, relationship with woman and relationship with his fellow men. Over intellectualism has destroyed intuitional and instinctive life. The mystery of life lies beyond the sway of the mind of man, his physical and natural self. Therefore Lawrence advocates relying on one's impulse and intuitions in realising the three aforesaid relationships and through this to realize oneself. He, therefore sets his faith in RELIGION OF THE BLOOD.

The non-intellectual orientation towards life so strongly advocated by him is not surprising for Lawrence strongly believed in the Dark Mystery of life and he saw all living forms instinct incarnate in it. The Dark Mystery cannot be known by intellect, it kills it in the very process of grasping it. Moreover the wide area of life is inaccessible to the intellect but may be known through instinct and intuition. The blood, the physical and natural self of man as it were catches the resource made by the mystery of life, and so brings life close to life itself. Objective reality and scientific facts had little meaning for Lawrence it corroborated by the dictates of the blood. Huxley writes when Lawrence was told about the theory of evolution of the universe and its evidences, he replied "But I don't care about evidence. Evidence does not mean anything to me, I don't feel it here. And he pressed his two hands to his solar plexus." He repeatedly wrote that man knows not only with his mind but also with a host of ganglis and solar plexus and what he knows thereby constitutes the real knowledge.

Lawrence believes in the Dark Mysterious God and rejects Christianity, because the Dark Mysterious God could be realised by the blood consciousness whereas Christianity stands for the denial of the flesh as something unholy. He once wrote:

> The magnificent here and now is the flesh—in ours and ours alone, and ours only for a time. We aught to dance with rapture and we should live in the flesh, and part of the living incarnate consciousness.

It is apparent that Lawrence rates the demand of the flesh as more exerting, and relegates a position of subordination to all moral and intellectual urges. He deplored the modern dualism, the setting up of dividing barriers between body and mind, between brain and blood, and protested against the gray misanthropy which seeks to make the body.

In a world materialistic and modernized with science and technology he felt life was full of dead modes of living made him turn away, for he was convinced that everything connected with it was evil, and everything opposing it was good, this naturally led to a different way of thinking and formulate a philosophy particularly that which expresses itself as a philosophy of Two Worlds.

During Dante's time two views were prevalent in Florence that came to be popularly known as Neri and Bianci—Black and White, Dark and Light. It was an old way to divide the world into Body and Spirit,

Below and Above. In Phaedrus, Plato speaks of it as a team of two horses—White and Black—driven by a charioteer.

The White horse is the right hand upright, is a lover of all virtues like honesty, modesty, temperance, and the follower of true glory. Whereas the Black is crooked, flat faced and dark. There is no doubt which might have been Plato's choice.

To Socrates and Pythagoras, the symbol of life growing in oneself was the image of the spirit rising upright which was later adopted by Christianity and other Idealists. The term used to describe sublime, lofty exalted, enlightenment, climbing higher and higher. To Lawrence these imageries is the language of everything he hates in the world. He reversed, therefore Dark comes instead. Dark, Dark, Dark. He reverse Plato. The novelty of this reversed idealism and the fact that the Two World philosophy wants one to have their world and desire for the other.

Plato's Charioteer was the Ideas, Lawrence first left in unnamed, till later he began to call it the thing between the two worlds, the Infinite between the two Absolutes. Later he began to call it God, and finally named it the Dark God.

There is nothing new about an anti-intellectual philosophy or boasting of the unconscious. His hatred of Ideas "like the nail struck into the bark of a growing tree" is put more powerfully by Schopenhauer as illustrated in the proposition that Ideas are only substitutes. He was one of the haters of reason which Socrates used to make fun of calling them misologists. And his cracking 'dark races' is the 'Noble Savage'. All intellectuals right from Kant belittled the intellect. And the emphasis he lays on the importance and acceptance of the body, is explicitly stated in Nietzsche, and more magnified in Whitman. That Christianity's values are worn out was already expressed in six pages by Blake. The concept of God in terms of modern experience, Middleton Murray had already made an absorbing record of it. Most of his opinion about life has been discussed, demonstrated in books, article and lectures for many decades in two continents by Count Herman. His conclusions are nothing but mere agreement or disagreement which had themselves risen in the same way. But what makes a study of his philosophy interesting is that instead of his philosophy being a clue to Lawrence, it is Lawrence who is a clue to his philosophy which becomes an important part of the general meaning of his whole work.

DUALITY: "A central feature Lawrence's thought is its dualism" writes H.M. Dalaski. In *The Forked Flame: Reflection on the Death of a Porcupine* Lawrence proclaims his duality:

> I knew I was composed of two waves.... I am framed in the struggle and embrace of waves, of the two opposites of darkness and light but also asserts that everything that exists even a stone has two sides to its nature. He regards duality, this duality as an all pervading principle of life, and experiences it symbolically in terms of the dark and light, the flesh and the spirit, the eagle and the dove, the tiger and the lamb, lion and the unicorn. But as he expounds this principle of the existence of conflicting forces, he also emphasizes that the opposition between them must never be ended, for the end of this opposition would be the end of life itself.

How is the conflict between to be resolved? Lawrence suggests that it lies not in its merger but in the external balance between them. "The two infinitives—negative and positive that are always related but never identical. They are always opposites, but there exists a relation between them.... To say that the two are one this is an inadmissible lie. The two are not merged but integrated and still in a state of tension. Life sustaining and life creating forbidding for ever the merger of the opposites maintaining both in a state of mutual complimentary balance."

Lawrence views relationship between the individual and the external world in much the same way. An individual if he wants to realise his complete self, it is essential for him to expand and get involved with the external universe, but this involvement does not imply its obliteration of the self or a complete defiance of the external universe. For an ideal relationship the self and the external universe have to be held in perfect balance.

This principle assumes a still greater importance when the relationship is between a man and a woman. In this case "there is a double reconciliation of opposites" for the man and the woman are required not only to meet the opposites, but to reconcile the opposing qualities within themselves. The relationship is envisaged as a meeting on equal terms of two who have achieved their full individuality, and transcend their duality is the balance that is attained between them. Lawrence gives this balance even a religious sanctity "If it has to be life then it has to be fifty percent me, fifty percent thee. And the third thing the spark that springs from this balance is timeless. Jesus who saw it a bit vaguely called it the Holy Ghost. Between men and women fifty percent me fifty percent woman then the pure spark. Either this or less than nothing."

The principle of duality runs through all his novels. In *Sons and Lovers* the happiness of Walter Morel is wrecked by his wife Gertrude when she tries to 'civilize' her husband according to her middle class standard

> The pity was she was too much his opposite, she could not be content with the little that he might be. She would have him the much that he aught to be. So in seeking to make him nobler than he could be she destroys him.

And the reason why the relation between Paul and Miriam fail is that Miriam "wants to absorb, absorb as if you must fill yourself up with love, because you've got a shortage somewhere".

In *Women in Love* Gudrun destroys Gerald Crick through her desire to domesticate him. Whereas Ursula and Birkin find fulfillment since the two respect the divine otherness of each other and do not aim at unnatural domination.

As Lawrence grew up he was convinced that the relation between men and women was one of conflict, not a natural expression of harmony. He had observed his parents relationship, an ill matched couple. His father was a miner, with no pretension, no pride no respectability, half educated, drunkard and slightly brutal, sullen. His mother, charming, superior and a lady like. Lawrence was against his father, he hated him, his ways and his pit darkness. He and his mother formed a league against him. Finding her marriage not being to her expectation she was drawn to Lawrence. The strain this insipid relationship imposed on his adolescent mind can be seen in his abnormal sensitivity to any threatened domination of women was the main reason for human unhappiness, along was this was the economic disequilibrium to the violation of male supremacy and sexual harmony. This line of thought led him to glorify the primitive state which he believed was based on the knowledge of the comic laws underlying sexual relationship.

His tirade against women was fierce. He considered the modern civilized women an enemy to men. Robbing him of his greatest possession manhood, his masculinity and bringing him under the dominance and control of her will. In *Aaron Rod* he writes "I hate her, when she knows and when she wills, I hate her when she will make of me that which serves her desire. She may love me, she may be kind and soft to me. She may give her life for me, but why, only I am hers." "Women are the hottest hell. Once they set the start of you, there's nothing they would do to you, once they have got you." As a novelist who used the gift of sensational immediacy to make vivid "A life thought adventure" (as he called it) which is unique in literature.

Exaltation of Sex—T.S. Eliot in *After Strange Gods* writes "no one was less a sensualist than Lawrence. The fact that he believes that sex is a primary fact of life and an undeniable reality. He treated it with holy reverence that needed no unnatural secrecy about it. He believed in a kind of sex mysticism. The experience of sex is the experience of the Infinite:

> To him sex the way a woman fulfills her being, and man one of his chief creative function for which reason he always extolled marriage. But the sexual experience was also a door to a new realm of consciousness an initiation into the divine mystic, the mystery of the other world that is close behind.

In *The Rainbow,* Tom and Lydia come together after a period of estrangement:

> It was an entry into another circle of existence, it was the baptism of another life.
>
> It was the complete confirmation. Their feet thread strange gravels of knowledge, their footsteps were lit up with discovery, and always the light of the transfiguration burned in their hearts. He went his way as before. She went her way to the rest of the world there seemed no change. But God had taken His abode with them....

In *Women in Love,* he declares the marriage of Birkin and Ursula:

> This marriage with her was his resurrection, his life. It was something beyond love, such a gladness of having surpassed oneself, of having transcended the old existence.

In this transcendental view of sex Lawrence may be compared to Kierkegaard who writes "And God the Father, the Inscrutable, the Unknowable, We know in the flesh of a Woman."

In *Fantasia of the Unconscious* Lawrence carefully distinguishes between the higher and lower phases of being conscious, the sensual and spiritual aspects of sex that should be held important. He condemns Freud and other psychologists who make sex the basis of every human activities. "The psycho-analysts driving us back to the sexual consummation always doing us infinite damage," and in Chapter IX of the same book he writes:

> When man loses his deep sense of purposive creative activity, he feels lost and is lost. When he makes his sexual consummation even in his secret soul, he falls into the beginning of despair.... With sex as the most accepted prime motive the world drifts into despair and anarchy.

This clearly shows that sex as understood by Lawrence is much above gross animality and his novels adequately express his hatred of animality.

Lawrence was outraged to find that sex which is the primary fact of life and an undeniable reality was treated more often than not as a dirty thing, as something that should not be mentioned in polite society. This attitude of keeping sex as secret thing destroyed the holy reverence the primitives had. Lawrence's attitude is deeply rooted in what Colin Wilson calls 'sexual mysticism'. In other words he believed that the deepest mysteries of life can be known through sex, it is important to a complete and organic life. F.R. Leavis sums up "Life is fulfilled in the individual, nowhere, but in a true marital relation which is creative more than the sense of producing children." Only through sex one can fulfill and gain the insight into the mysterious essence of things, otherwise in Lawrence's words "Seen from this angle sex is not merely a functional act but creative act revealing of life and the beauty of being alive."

Lawrence could never forget, as most forget the dark presence of the 'otherness' that lies beyond the boundaries of man's mind. The special sensibility was accompanied by a prodigious power of rendering the immediately experienced 'other' in terms of literary art. Lawrence wrote from within, the man the woman, the love the mind. There is a always a strong autobiographical element in his novels. He projects his novels the very centre of his own personal experience, so that they set out sometimes fiercely, sometimes desperately his deepest insight and forms of awareness, the lyric and the dramatic mode interpenetrate.

His attitude to sex is fundamentally different from that of others. He exalts it to a spiritual level. In the words of Huxley "for Lawrence the significance of the sexual experience was that in the immediate non-mental knowledge of the divine otherness, is brought in to speak, to a focus—a focus of darkness.

Lawrence wanted to use novel as a means of conveying his philosophy of life. That Lawrence was a prophetic writer cannot be denied. As Stuart Sherman once said "His novels don't leave you where they found you.

They have designs upon you. But when the preacher runs away with the artist the result is lamentable." But Jascha Kessler's essay "Descent in Darkness" writes when the prophetic side is best realised as in *The Rainbow. Women in Love* that his works are most successful." In D.H. Lawrence: *The Prophet of the Midlands* (1951) Vivian de Sola Pinto finds that Lawrence was not the kind of prophetic "who foretells what will happen in the future, though he may do that incidentally, but who tells forth the literal meaning of the Greek words, a great living truth which comes from the depth of his being". To Prof. Pinto the best part of Lawrence's writings both in poetry and prose is in the great tradition of Langland, Bunyan, Blake, Ruskin and Morris.

Eliseo Vivas in *Failure and Triumph of Art* writes that Lawrence often imposes non-aesthetic demands on aesthetic experiences which form the substance of his novels. Lawrence distorts his creative vision to express his philosophical ideas. There is the presence of Lawrence the artist and Lawrence the philosopher puts across his message too prominently.

This view is shared by others too who are baffled by his insistence on doctrinal belief, find it difficult to come to terms philosopher. David Daiches did not include Lawrence in his illuminating book *The Novel and the Modern World* for he too was unable to come to terms with "the obsessed prophet did not know how to approach him or relate the two aspects of this genius". Harry T. Moore felt "Lawrence was not merely writing novels, stories and poems he was often through them recommending a way of life." Graham Hough writes "certain ideas can be distracted from the fiction of Lawrence, fiction and doctrine co-exist in all his major novels—what Lawrence offers is not a consistent philosophy but an understanding of his unique vision of life.... Lawrence was deeply committed to certain ideas and uses the novel form for their exposition." Lawrence the prophet gets better of Lawrence the artist and novelist is reduced to the level of propaganda literature.

Lawrence himself feels that the two selves of the writer—the artist and the philosopher might work counter to the inspiration of each other so that the troth of the one differs from the truth of the other. What the artist offers is an imaginatively lived aesthetic experience which adds to the awareness of life while the moralist tries to use the substance of a work of art for propagating ideas for speaking out his message. In such a case the intention of a work of art will clash with the intention of a writer.

F.R. Leavis in *D.H. Lawrence: The Novelist* views Lawrence first as an artist, though he did not ignore the prophetic side. Leavis considers Lawrence as an original philosopher which he was decidedly was not. His vision was deep and compelling. But his originality lay in his power of utterance. Lawrence in fact like Ruskin philosophy from the library and almirahs to the popular stream. The details of his doctrine are a blurred and rubbed and even partially forgotten. But the living part contribute to the living faith of a great number of people. Everyone who are disturbed by the sexual behaviour of their children are not shy of talking about it, are ready to consult a psychiatrist. No doubt the sexual behaviour of most literate person born after 1925 have been profoundly affected by his writings, have found Lawrence helping them dispel their apprehension and in making their sexual being the crowning enrichment of their emotional life, instead of feeling shameful or sordid opines Anthony West.

The combination of psychological realism and poetic intensity with which he presents his mystic of physical love has found admiration as well as criticism. At times the psycho-sexual details are overdone both betraying a diseased mind. His portrayal of the vital experiences of which the most important appears to be sexual relationship indicates that he is deeply conscious of their religious nature, so that though sex is frequently his theme it is handled as a sacred thing, spiritual not animal. And this as he himself clarifies remains true even in *Lady Chatterley's Lover*. Lawrence is the prophet of the primitive instinct and passion, his appeal is to the heart and not to the head. He seeks to persuade not by the reasoning faculty but by the emotional impact of his writing holds Albert. There is always a strong emotional element in his novels.

The line that divides literature from pornography is a thin one, Lawrence crossed it unhesitatingly. It has been said that the aggressive display of sexuality whatever be the explanation his novels reveal a vulgar minded exhibitionist. His mystical rhapsodies of the flesh does not enhance life, though he possessed the literary power.

Art to Lawrence as to Oscar Wilde is neither moral, immoral or amoral. A novel which is morally balanced makes a dull reading, if it reveals true, vivid relationship it is immoral work, and if it falsifies the matter it becomes amoral. Victorian prudery he did not care for. A hard cored puritan may call his novels sexy, obscene, cheap. But a puritan is himself a sick person. Lawrence used the novel for a serious person as Bernard Shaw used the drama, as a writer he was a genius, an iconoclast, who has shattered our belief and notions about sex. He is a philosopher with a message of his own. He rejects Christ and preaches a religion of flesh and blood—flesh being wiser than the spirit. He advocates the worship of a certain 'Dark God' in place of the Christian God.

His novels *Rainbow* and *Lady Chatterley's Lover* were banned as being pornographic, but later the world realized its mistake and conceded that Lawrence was giving a new religion of sex through his novels. He insists that the need of the body should not be ignored, spiritual fulfillment and salvation is possible only through a right kind of physical satisfaction. Like Acharya Rajneesh he advocates through sex beyond sex.

To Lawrence novel is one bright book of life "to be alive, to be man and alive, to be a whole man alive. This is the work—alive to the beauty, ugliness vast panorama of this variegated life". According to Baker "Lawrences novels are an exploration and exposition of the self."

As a novelist he has no imitators, as a prophet no successor. Whether he is a great writer or not, whether he is a true or false prophet little matters, but his works will always remain a massive phenomenon, and will have to be taken into account whether his ultimate reputation simply becomes a part of a general alteration of the mental and moral landscape or alteration that has been widely noticed but not adequately described.

As a novelist he yielded completely to his sensitive temperament. He belonged to the same order of Emily Bronte, a wild creature obeying instincts, fierce and gentle, passionate and submissive. He was a romantic whom circumstances compelled to behave like a realist. He was Christian driven into the camp of anti Christian, a moralist doomed to have his books condemned for immorality, an ordinary man trapped in a corner as a rebel and was forced to sustain that character. Never an original thinker stumbled upon certain ideas which were becoming current and clung to them tenaciously. An idea coldly expressed is a new thing when it turns into a conviction. Passionately lived with a few ideas, he became possessed and poured them forth in the torrent of his novels, poems and letters. The words in which he clothed them derive their quality from his sensitiveness to beauty and his emotional vitality.

WORKS CITED

Becket, Fiona. *The Complete Critical Guide to D.H. Lawrence*. University of Washington.

Carswell, Catherine. 'The Savage Pilgrimage'. Cambridge, CUP, 1932.

Dix, Carol. *D.H. Lawrence*. Macmillan, 1980.

Draper, R.P. *D.H. Lawrence Critical Heritage*. Psychology Press, 1997.

Ellis, David. *Women in Love, a Case Book*. Cambridge, CUP, 2006.

Femibough, Anne. *D.H. Lawrence Aesthetics and Ideology,* Oxford, Clarendon Press, 1993.

——— (ed). *Cambridge Companion to D.H. Lawrence*, Cambridge, Cambridge University Press, 2001.

Hough, Graham. *The Dark Sun—A Study of D.H. Lawrence*. Duckworth, 1956.

Kermode, Frank. *Lawrence*. London, 1973.

Lawrence, D.H. *Sons and Lovers*. Harper Collins, India, 2010.

———. *Women in Love*. Harper Collins, India, 2006.

———. *Lady Chatterley's Lover*. Harper Collins, India, 2013.

———. *Rainbow*. Penguin, India, 2002.

———. *Letters*. CUP.

Leavis, F.R. *D.H. Lawrence's Novels*. Chatto Windus, London, 1955.

Maclend, Shiela. *Lawrence's Men and Women*. Heinmann, London, 1965.

Moore, Harry T. *The Priest of Love, Life of D.H. Lawrence*, 1974.

Norman, Mailer. 'The Prisoner of Sex'. Harper Magazine, May 1971.

Terry, Eagleton. *The English Novel an Introduction*. Wiley Blackwell, 2005.

Weekes, Mark Kincard. *D.H. Lawrence Triumph to Exile*. Cambridge, CUP, 1996.

Trains in the Short Stories of Ruskin Bond

NORAH NIVEDITA SHAW

THERE is no doubt that the contribution of Railways and trains by the British indeed proved to be extremely heavenly blessing to India-clasped with beautiful studded gems of joys and romance. Who knows there might have been anti movements or revolts against the laying of railway tracks and bringing of the trains. For it is always said that the establishment of any new, big and positive set up faces varied challenges and confrontation from different corners. However the British were adamant not to look behind and did not deter from their gigantic goal.

The Indo-anglian as well as some English writers were deeply attracted towards the Indian Railway and have captured its essence in their works presenting either the small-town stations, at the time of the raj or the present day big city stations bursting at the seam. Trains or railway platforms form the background of their short stories or novels—be it Jules Verne through his well known novel *Around the World in Eighty Days* or the legendry writer and journalist Khuswant Singh in his epoch making novel on partition *Train to Pakistan*. A few other writers who have also made their mark revolving round the subject might be recalled as well—Jim Corbett, Rudyard Kipling, R.K. Laxman, Manoj Das, Flora Annie Steel, Intizar Husain, Satyajit Ray, Bil Aitken. A bird's eye view through most of the stories by the above-mentioned writers suggest that they do present trains or rail tracks or platforms in the background of their pieces but the fact is they remain merely as static background hardly empowering the story/work or becoming in any way wind-wings to propel the stories aptly. That is to say the events or the incidents, narrations or moments remain reminisces and could also have been there even without (except a few) mentioning the trains, compartments or platforms. However the only Indian writer who stands apart not only in style of presentation but bringing out an intense beauty, novelty and refreshing feel of delight through his varied works with trains or platforms as an integral part is none other than the living legend Ruskin Bond. Ruskin Bond has been living permanently amidst the beautiful surroundings of Mussorie (Landour) for more than seventy years. His bonding with the trains is old since the time he used to board alone to and fro from his boarding school BCS Shimla to Dehradoon. The varied themes in all his works have been brought forth with great perfection and have been rightly acclaimed worldwide. What is indeed remarkable has been their perpetual glaze of compassionate portrayal of love, loss, yearning and accomplishment, pain and struggle.

In the present paper I have scrutinized the artistic beauty and enchanting effect encompassing the train stories. The trains, railway platforms, compartments in the varied short stories of Bond become an integral part and are very much alive. They empower the characters completely adding unique charm and effect to the whole story.

'The Eyes Have It' is a very beautiful short story about two blind people who are travelling in a same compartment. Both of them pretend that they have eye sight without each other know about their blindness. The artistic beauty which brushes around the canvas could have been painted perfectly by Bond alone. The soothing colour of love and longing is brought out in a very natural way and impresses the reader completely. The piece grips the reader completely from beginning to the end and one reads it in one breathing.

The male protagonist is confident that his female co-passenger is not blind unlike him. On the other hand, even she assumes that she has been perfect in hiding her state of blindness. For when he deliberately enquires about the outside scene she retorts back—

> 'Why don't you look out of the window?' She asked.

The other interesting part of the story has been uniquely presented that is every man loves beautiful face. Here the hero while talking to the young girl effortlessly finds out that she has a pretty face. As soon as he boldly remarks:

> 'You have an interesting face' I remarked I was becoming quite daring, but it was a safe remark. Few girls can resist flattery. She laughed pleasantly—a clear, ringing laugh.
>
> 'It's nice to be told that I have an interesting face. I am tired of people telling me I have a pretty face.'
>
> Oh, so you do have a pretty face, thought I:....

The romance of two people meeting by chance only for a short while and the lingering of after affect of that brief and magical spell is re-enforced again and again in most of Bond's stories as well as novellas.

However that fleeting moment in the short journeys particularly in the trains is picturized powerfully. Ruskin observes:

> …and I find that in my stories I wrote I the 1950's (when I was in my teens and in my twenties) there is a good deal of romance, often associated with trains. People are always travelling in them and going all over the place, but just occasionally two people meet, their paths cross, and though they may part again, quite soon (…) their lives have been changed in some indefinable way.

In the above-mentioned short story, 'The Eyes Have It', also the hero is prepared to remain there sitting with her for almost 'any length of time', 'to listen to her talking'. Bond's words become not only poetic but also spray its romantic beauty over us once more enhancing our belief in love and joy and true wisdom.

> Her voice had the sparkle of a mountain stream. As soon as she left the train, she would forget our brief encounter; but it would stay with me for the rest of the journey, and for some time after.

It's only after the unknown girl has left the train having reached her final destination, when another new passenger who has boarded the train and occupying the same place, informs the protagonist with an interrogation:

> …'It was her eyes I noticed, not her hair. She had beautiful eyes— but they were of no use to her. She was completely blind. Didn't you notice?'

Professor Meena G. Khorana in her complete research on Ruskin Bond for more than fifteen years remarks:

> The story is full of verbal ironies: the protagonist thinks she cannot see that he is blind because he is sitting in a dark corner and because he can call on his memories and other senses to carry on an intelligent conversation; and she does not know that he does not know she is blind. The story also comments on "seeing", because many people who have good eyesight do not have the ability, or the time, to notice details.

The other story which is a bit different in matter that is there is absence of young man-woman relationship, 'The Woman on Platform 8'. The short story relates to the compassion and love shown by an unknown woman towards a young boy boarding the train all alone by himself. This particular piece has touched me immensely. The young boy reminding us of the young Ruskin (as a boy) is compelled to manage alone on a railway platform to change train 'on his way to boarding school'. This story was written by Bond remembering his childhood days when he 'spent a great deal of time on them' (railway platforms) 'waiting for connecting trains to Kalka or Saharanpur or Barrackpore or Rajkot'. However once again Ruskin Bond does not leave the focal point. The theme remains the same, brief meeting 'of strangers' 'on a train or platform and touching each other's lives forever'. Again I am reminded of Prof. Meena G. Khorana's view and completely agree with her view that though Bond's themes are repeated again and again yet there is no monotony. This repetition of characters and themes and story element or patterns over and over again in most of his short stories or novellas or novels without being monotonous can only be seen in Bond's works. There lies the beauty of a great artist.

The above-mentioned unique piece captures the loneliness and insecurity of a young boy waiting at Ambala station for his connecting train. He happens to meet an extremely 'loving woman on the platform' 9. This woman is caring and has great compassion for the lonesome boy. She not only feeds Arun, but gives him company and more than that though for a short while adopts him. When Satish, another student of the same boarding school and his mother arrive at the platform, this unknown woman deliberately 'tells a white lie that she is Arun's mother'. I in my research on Ruskin Bond published in the year 2008, *Ruskin Bond of India: A True Son of the Soil* enlighten strongly:

> Nevertheless this lie is the climax of the story. Initially amazed.... While Arun reconciles himself and accepts the lie as a vital truth.

When Satish's mother observes about the danger for a young boy to be all alone on big stations where 'there are so many suspicious characters hanging about', the 'surrogate mother of Arun' immediately comes to his rescue:

> 'Arun can travel alone though', said the woman beside me, and somehow I felt grateful to her for saying that. I had already forgiven her for lying: and besides, 'I had taken an instinctive dislike to Satish's mother.'

The third and the last story with railways as the backbone is undoubtedly the famous romantic short story is the famous *The Night Train at Deoli* admired by the youngsters. In fact the stories written during the 1950's have been published collectively under the Penguins rightly titled *The Night Train at Deoli and Other Stories*. This story was first published by *The Illustrated Weekly* in 1957-58. It is very powerful short piece grasping and portraying the magical moment in a very natural and artistic manner. As usual Ruskin mesmerizes us with his unique skill bringing out a simple and common incident of a young college going boy returning to his granny's home during summer vacation. He comes across a young and charming girl on a platform of a small and unknown town, Deoli. The girl is selling flowers in a cane basket. Though she is poor yet she is graceful in her bearing. The narrator or the young boy is instantly attracted towards the girl:

> When she came to my window, she stopped. She saw that I was looking at her intently, but at first she pretended not to notice. She had a pale skin, set off by shiny black hair, and dark, troubled eyes. And then those eyes, searching and eloquent, met mine.

The whole incident is very simple and common 'and one which can happen with anyone', is however conveyed with intense depth and unique imagination. The language is very simple yet speaks volumes.

The background of the railways and the scenes around coming in preview of the moving trains has excellently perfectly empowered which not only the characters but the readers as well.

> I watched her as the platform slipped away. She was alone on the platform and she did not move, but she was looking at me and smiling. I watched her until the signal-box came in the way, and then the jungle hid the station, but I could see her standing there alone....

Such an insignificant and irrelevant event is likely to vanish away as soon as one reaches one's destination. The same happens with the narrator or the protagonist. The story grips the reader with its new charm and interest when the narrator or the protagonist returning to his college after long vacation is once again crossing the same station. The novelty lies in the fact that not only the young hero is 'keenly on the lookout for the girl' selling basket but the readers as well. He feels an unexpected thrill when he sees her 'walking up the platform'. The use of fine words and the rare style which Bond adopts is indeed remarkable. Let us observe the following description:

> I was looking out for her as the train drew into the station, and I felt an unexpected thrill when I saw her walking up the platform. I sprang off the foot-board and waved to her.
>
> When she saw me, she smiled. She was pleased that I remembered her. I was pleased that, she remembered me. We were both pleased, and it was almost like a meeting of old friends.

And further the deep emotional feeling is put forth very strongly though in simple and beautiful words:

> I felt the impulse to put her on the train there and then, and take her away with me; I could not bear the thought of having to watch her recede into the distance of Deoli station. I took the baskets from her hand and put them down on the ground. She put out her hand for one of them, but I caught her hand and held it.

The story goes on. The narrator eagerly waits for the closure of the college term to meet the girl but this time the girl is not there. In spite of continuous effort, the narrator is unable to know her whereabouts. It is impossible for a youth to bear such a loss. However, he 'feels tenderness' and a certain sense 'of responsibility' towards her and 'vows to break his journey some day to make enquiries—but he never does'. No other writer could be so optimist turning the whole instance of sorrow with glowing waves of hope. The story concludes beautifully:

> But I will never break my journey there. It may spoil my game. I prefer to keep hoping and dreaming and looking out of the window up and down that lonely platform, waiting for the girl with the baskets.
>
> I never break my journey at Deoli, but I pass through as often as I can.

Bond continues his long journey as a writer for more than seventy years now perhaps still looking out of his small window from his top hill small house, dreaming and hoping without breaking his journey.

Today the world is pacing very fast, the people (who are able to afford) prefer plains to trains or other means of transportation. However the essence of joy and romance, travelling by the trains still remains unmatched—when we can ponder, stand and stare from a distance at our lives and come to know ourselves completely.

WORKS CITED

Bond, Ruskin (Edited). *The Penguin Book of Indian Railway Stories.* Penguin, 1994.

———. *The Night Train at Deoli and Other Stories.* Penguin, 1988.

———. *Scenes From a Writer's Life: A Memoir*. Penguin, New Delhi, 1997.

Khorana, Meena G. *The Life And Works of Ruskin Bond.* Praeger, London, 2003.

Shaw, Norah Nivedita. *Ruskin Bond of India: A True Son of the Soil.* Atlantic, 2008.